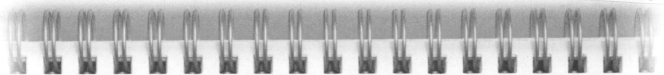

# Interactive Notebooks

## Grade 2

**Credits**

Content Editors: Elise Craver, Christine M. Schwab, Angela Triplett

Visit *carsondellosa.com* for correlations to Common Core, state, national, and Canadian provincial standards.

Carson-Dellosa Publishing, LLC
PO Box 35665
Greensboro, NC 27425 USA
carsondellosa.com

978-1-4838-2463-5
02-191157784

# Table of Contents

# What Are Interactive Notebooks?

Interactive notebooks are a unique form of note taking. Teachers guide students through creating pages of notes on new topics. Instead of being in the traditional linear, handwritten format, notes are colorful and spread across the pages. Notes also often include drawings, diagrams, and 3-D elements to make the material understandable and relevant. Students are encouraged to complete their notebook pages in ways that make sense to them. With this personalization, no two pages are exactly the same.

Because of their creative nature, interactive notebooks allow students to be active participants in their own learning. Teachers can easily differentiate pages to address the levels and needs of each learner. The notebooks are arranged sequentially, and students can create tables of contents as they create pages, making it simple for students to use their notebooks for reference throughout the year. The interactive, easily personalized format makes interactive notebooks ideal for engaging students in learning new concepts.

Using interactive notebooks can take as much or as little time as you like. Students will initially take longer to create pages but will get faster as they become familiar with the process of creating pages. You may choose to only create a notebook page as a class at the beginning of each unit, or you may choose to create a new page for each topic within a unit. You can decide what works best for your students and schedule.

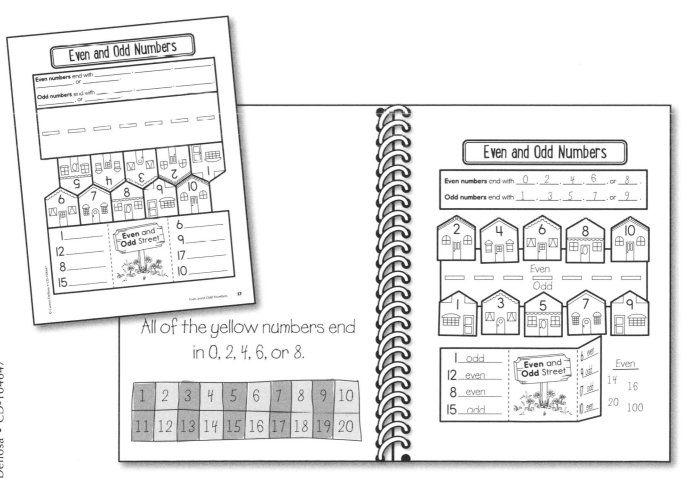

A student's interactive notebook for even and odd numbers

# Getting Started

You can start using interactive notebooks at any point in the school year. Use the following guidelines to help you get started in your classroom. (For more specific details, management ideas, and tips, see page 10.)

### 1. Plan each notebook.

Use the planning template (page 9) to lay out a general plan for the topics you plan to cover in each notebook for the year.

### 2. Choose a notebook type.

Interactive notebooks are usually either single-subject, spiral-bound notebooks, composition books, or three-ring binders with loose-leaf paper. Each type presents pros and cons. See page 5 for a more in-depth look at each type of notebook.

### 3. Allow students to personalize their notebooks.

Have students decorate their notebook covers, as well as add their names and subjects. This provides a sense of ownership and emphasizes the personalized nature of the notebooks.

### 4. Number the pages and create the table of contents.

Have students number the bottom outside corner of each page, front and back. When completing a new page, adding a table of contents entry will be easy. Have students title the first page of each notebook "Table of Contents." Have them leave several blank pages at the front of each notebook for the table of contents. Refer to your general plan for an idea of about how many entries students will be creating.

### 5. Start creating pages.

Always begin a new page by adding an entry to the table of contents. Create the first notebook pages along with students to model proper format and expectations.

This book contains individual topics for you to introduce. Use the pages in the order that best fits your curriculum. You may also choose to alter the content presented to better match your school's curriculum. The provided lesson plans often do not instruct students to add color. Students should make their own choices about personalizing the content in ways that make sense to them. Encourage students to highlight and color the pages as they desire while creating them.

After introducing topics, you may choose to add more practice pages. Use the reproducibles (pages 78–96) to easily create new notebook pages for practice or to introduce topics not addressed in this book.

Use the grading rubric (page 11) to grade students' interactive notebooks at various points throughout the year. Provide students copies of the rubric to glue into their notebooks and refer to as they create pages.

# What Type of Notebook Should I Use?

## Spiral Notebook

*The pages in this book are formatted for a standard one-subject notebook.*

**Pros**

- Notebook can be folded in half.
- Page size is larger.
- It is inexpensive.
- It often comes with pockets for storing materials.

**Cons**

- Pages can easily fall out.
- Spirals can snag or become misshapen.
- Page count and size vary widely.
- It is not as durable as a binder.

**Tips**

- Encase the spiral in duct tape to make it more durable.
- Keep the notebooks in a central place to prevent them from getting damaged in desks.

## Composition Notebook

**Pros**

- Pages don't easily fall out.
- Page size and page count are standard.
- It is inexpensive.

**Cons**

- Notebook cannot be folded in half.
- Page size is smaller.
- It is not as durable as a binder.

**Tips**

- Copy pages meant for standard-sized notebooks at 85 or 90 percent. Test to see which works better for your notebook.

## Binder with Loose-Leaf Paper

**Pros**

- Pages can be easily added, moved, or removed.
- Pages can be removed individually for grading.
- You can add full-page printed handouts.
- It has durable covers.

**Cons**

- Pages can easily fall out.
- Pages aren't durable.
- It is more expensive than a notebook.
- Students can easily misplace or lose pages.
- Larger size makes it more difficult to store.

**Tips**

- Provide hole reinforcers for damaged pages.

# How to Organize an Interactive Notebook

You may organize an interactive notebook in many different ways. You may choose to organize it by unit and work sequentially through the book. Or, you may choose to create different sections that you will revisit and add to throughout the year. Choose the format that works best for your students and subject.

An interactive notebook includes different types of pages in addition to the pages students create. Non-content pages you may want to add include the following:

## Title Page

This page is useful for quickly identifying notebooks. It is especially helpful in classrooms that use multiple interactive notebooks for different subjects. Have students write the subject (such as "Math") on the title page of each interactive notebook. They should also include their full names. You may choose to have them include other information such as the teacher's name, classroom number, or class period.

## Table of Contents

The table of contents is an integral part of the interactive notebook. It makes referencing previously created pages quick and easy for students. Make sure that students leave several pages at the beginning of each notebook for a table of contents.

## Expectations and Grading Rubric

It is helpful for each student to have a copy of the expectations for creating interactive notebook pages. You may choose to include a list of expectations for parents and students to sign, as well as a grading rubric (page 11).

## Unit Title Pages

Consider using a single page at the beginning of each section to separate it. Title the page with the unit name. Add a tab (page 78) to the edge of the page to make it easy to flip to the unit. Add a table of contents for only the pages in that unit.

## Glossary

Reserve a six-page section at the back of the notebook where students can create a glossary. Draw a line to split in half the front and back of each page, creating 24 sections. Combine Q and R and Y and Z to fit the entire alphabet. Have students add an entry as each new vocabulary word is introduced.

## Formatting Student Notebook Pages

The other major consideration for planning an interactive notebook is how to treat the left and right sides of a notebook spread. Interactive journals are usually viewed with the notebook open flat. This creates a left side and a right side. You have several options for how to treat the two sides of the spread.

Traditionally, the right side is used for the teacher-directed part of the lesson, and the left side is used for students to interact with the lesson content. The lessons in this book use this format. However, you may prefer to switch the order for your class so that the teacher-directed learning is on the left and the student input is on the right.

It can also be important to include standards, learning objectives, or essential questions in interactive notebooks. You may choose to write these on the top-left side of each page before completing the teacher-directed page on the right side. You may also choose to have students include the "Introduction" part of each lesson in that same top-left section. This is the *in, through, out* method. Students enter *in* the lesson on the top left of the page, go *through* the lesson on the right page, and exit *out* of the lesson on the bottom left with a reflection activity.

The following chart details different types of items and activities that you could include on each side.

| Left Side<br>Student Output | Right Side<br>Teacher-Directed Learning |
|---|---|
| • learning objectives<br>• essential questions<br>• I Can statements<br>• brainstorming<br>• making connections<br>• summarizing<br>• making conclusions<br>• practice problems<br>• opinions<br>• questions<br>• mnemonics<br>• drawings and diagrams | • vocabulary and definitions<br>• mini-lessons<br>• folding activities<br>• steps in a process<br>• example problems<br>• notes<br>• diagrams<br>• graphic organizers<br>• hints and tips<br>• big ideas |

Making a general plan for interactive notebooks will help with planning, grading, and testing throughout the year. You do not need to plan every single page, but knowing what topics you will cover and in what order can be helpful in many ways.

Use the Interactive Notebook Plan (page 9) to plan your units and topics and where they should be placed in the notebooks. Remember to include enough pages at the beginning for the non-content pages, such as the title page, table of contents, and grading rubric. You may also want to leave a page at the beginning of each unit to place a mini table of contents for just that section.

In addition, when planning new pages, it can be helpful to sketch the pieces you will need to create. Use the following notebook template and notes to plan new pages.

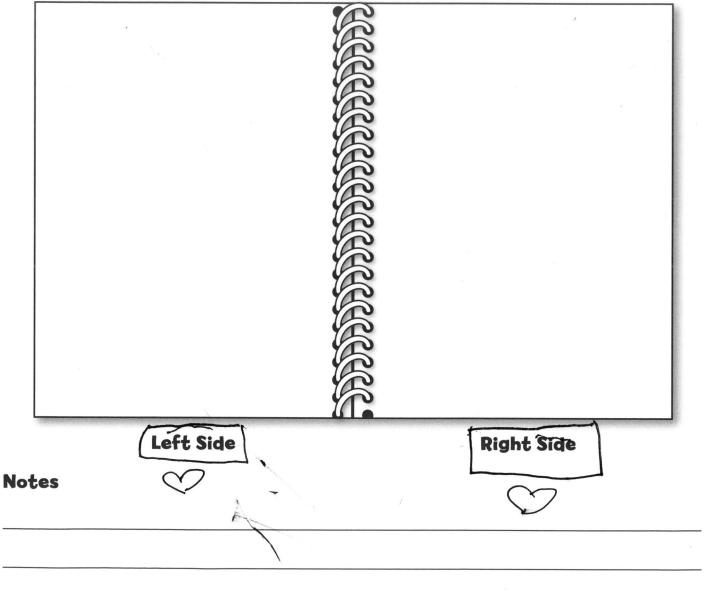

Left Side

Right Side

**Notes**

# Interactive Notebook Plan

| Page | Topic | Page | Topic |
|------|-------|------|-------|
| 1 | 1 | 51 | |
| 2 | 2 | 52 | |
| 3 | 3 | 53 | |
| 4 | 4 | 54 | |
| 5 | 5 | 55 | |
| 6 | 6 | 56 | |
| 7 | 7 | 57 | |
| 8 | 8 | 58 | |
| 9 | 9 | 59 | |
| 10 | 10 | 60 | |
| 11 | 11 | 61 | |
| 12 | 12 | 62 | |
| 13 | 13 | 63 | |
| 14 | 14 | 64 | |
| 15 | 15 | 65 | |
| 16 | 16 | 66 | |
| 17 | 17 | 67 | |
| 18 | 18 | 68 | |
| 19 | 19 | 69 | |
| 20 | 20 | 70 | |
| 21 | | 71 | |
| 22 | | 72 | |
| 23 | | 73 | |
| 24 | | 74 | |
| 25 | | 75 | |
| 26 | | 76 | |
| 27 | | 77 | |
| 28 | | 78 | |
| 29 | | 79 | |
| 30 | | 80 | |
| 31 | | 81 | |
| 32 | | 82 | |
| 33 | | 83 | |
| 34 | | 84 | |
| 35 | | 85 | |
| 36 | | 86 | |
| 37 | | 87 | |
| 38 | | 88 | |
| 39 | | 89 | |
| 40 | | 90 | |
| 41 | | 91 | |
| 42 | | 92 | |
| 43 | | 93 | |
| 44 | | 94 | |
| 45 | | 95 | |
| 46 | | 96 | |
| 47 | | 97 | |
| 48 | | 98 | |
| 49 | | 99 | |
| 50 | | 100 | |

# Managing Interactive Notebooks in the Classroom

## Working with Younger Students

- Use your yearly plan to preprogram a table of contents that you can copy and give to students to glue into their notebooks, instead of writing individual entries.

- Have assistants or parent volunteers precut pieces.

- Create glue sponges to make gluing easier. Place large sponges in plastic containers with white glue. The sponges will absorb the glue. Students can wipe the backs of pieces across the sponges to apply the glue with less mess.

## Creating Notebook Pages

- For storing loose pieces, add a pocket to the inside back cover. Use the envelope pattern (page 81), an envelope, or a resealable plastic bag. Or, tape the bottom and side edges of the two last pages of the notebook together to create a large pocket.

- When writing under flaps, have students trace the outline of each flap so that they can visualize the writing boundary.

- Where the dashed line will be hidden on the inside of the fold, have students first fold the piece in the opposite direction so that they can see the dashed line. Then, students should fold the piece back the other way along the same fold line to create the fold in the correct direction.

- To avoid losing pieces, have students keep all of their scraps on their desks until they have finished each page.

- To contain paper scraps and avoid multiple trips to the trash can, provide small groups with small buckets or tubs.

- For students who run out of room, keep full and half sheets available. Students can glue these to the bottom of the pages and fold them up when not in use.

## Dealing with Absences

- Create a model notebook for absent students to reference when they return to school.

- Have students cut a second set of pieces as they work on their own pages.

## Using the Notebook

- To organize sections of the notebook, provide each student with a sheet of tabs (page 78).

- To easily find the next blank page, either cut off the top-right corner of each page as it is used or attach a long piece of yarn or ribbon to the back cover to be used as a bookmark.

# Interactive Notebook Grading Rubric

| 4 | _____ Table of contents is complete.<br>_____ All notebook pages are included.<br>_____ All notebook pages are complete.<br>_____ Notebook pages are neat and organized.<br>_____ Information is correct.<br>_____ Pages show personalization, evidence of learning, and original ideas. |
|---|---|
| **3** | _____ Table of contents is mostly complete.<br>_____ One notebook page is missing.<br>_____ Notebook pages are mostly complete.<br>_____ Notebook pages are mostly neat and organized.<br>_____ Information is mostly correct.<br>_____ Pages show some personalization, evidence of learning, and original ideas. |
| **2** | _____ Table of contents is missing a few entries.<br>_____ A few notebook pages are missing.<br>_____ A few notebook pages are incomplete.<br>_____ Notebook pages are somewhat messy and unorganized.<br>_____ Information has several errors.<br>_____ Pages show little personalization, evidence of learning, or original ideas. |
| **1** | _____ Table of contents is incomplete.<br>_____ Many notebook pages are missing.<br>_____ Many notebook pages are incomplete.<br>_____ Notebook pages are too messy and unorganized to use.<br>_____ Information is incorrect.<br>_____ Pages show no personalization, evidence of learning, or original ideas. |

# Solving Word Problems

## Introduction

Give each student a word problem, such as *Last year Juan had 20 fish. Now, Juan has 16 fish. Yesterday, he gave 5 of them to his cousin. How many fish does Juan have left?* Read the problem aloud. Ask students to circle all of the numbers in the problem. Have them study the circled numbers and place an X on any numbers they do not need. Ask students if this is a subtraction or addition problem. Have them circle the clues or key words (*left*). Then, have students draw pictures to represent the parts of the word problem. Finally, have them write number sentences and solve for the answer.

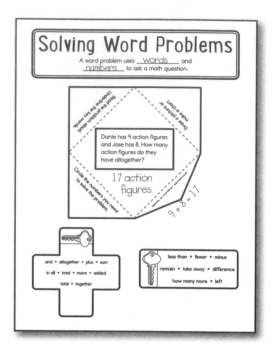

## Creating the Notebook Page

Guide students through the following steps to complete the right-hand page in their notebooks.

1. Add a Table of Contents entry for the Solving Word Problems pages.

2. Cut out the title and glue it to the top of the page.

3. Complete the sentence. (A word problem uses **words** and **numbers** to ask a math question.)

4. Cut out the word problem strategies flap book. Apply glue to the back of the center square and attach it below the title so that it is oriented as a square.

5. Cut out the word problem. Glue it to the middle section of the flap book.

6. Read the word problem and follow the strategies on each corner flap. Under each flap, write the information gained or explain how this strategy helped.

7. Cut out the plus and minus signs and glue them below the flap book. Discuss the key words on each and how they can be used as clues when solving word problems. Find the key word in the word problem and highlight it.

8. Use all of the information you gathered about the problem to solve for the answer. Write the answer in the center of the flap book.

## Reflect on Learning

To complete the left-hand page, have students write their own word problems. Have students exchange notebooks with partners and solve each other's word problems.

# Solving Word Problems

A word problem uses _____ and _____ to ask a math question.

Read the problem aloud. Underline the key words.

Draw a picture or make a chart.

Circle the numbers you need to solve the problem.

Write a number sentence.

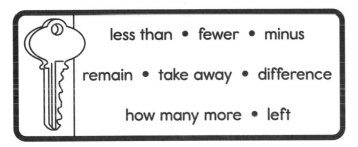

less than • fewer • minus

remain • take away • difference

how many more • left

and • altogether • plus • sum

in all • more • added

total • together

Dante has 9 action figures and Jose has 8. How many action figures do they have altogether?

# Mental Math

## Introduction

Write the problem *18 – 9* on the board. Ask students to solve the problem in their heads without using paper or fingers. Ask students who found the correct answer to explain how they solved the problem. Write their strategies on the board. Tell students that there are many different strategies to solve math problems.

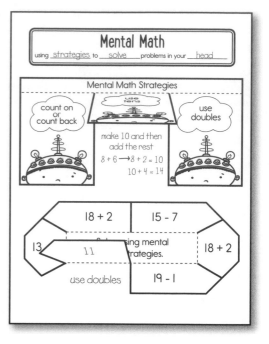

## Creating the Notebook Page

Guide students through the following steps to complete the right-hand page in their notebooks.

1. Add a Table of Contents entry for the Mental Math pages.

2. Cut out the title and glue it to the top of the page.

3. Complete the definition (using **strategies** to **solve** problems in your **head**).

4. Cut out the *Mental Math Strategies* flap book. Cut on the solid lines to create three flaps. Apply glue to the back of the top section and attach it below the title.

5. Discuss the strategy on each flap with a partner. Then, write an explanation of each strategy in your own words under the flap.

6. Cut out the octangonal flap book. Cut on the solid lines to create six flaps. Apply glue to the back of the center section and attach it to the bottom of the page.

7. Mentally solve each problem using one of the three strategies and write the answer on the underside of the flap. Under the flap, write which strategy you used to solve it.

## Reflect on Learning

To complete the left-hand page, have students write three addition problems and three subtraction problems. Have students exchange notebooks with partners and place the notebooks facedown. Set a timer. Have students quickly flip over their notebooks and use strategies to mentally solve each problem, one at a time. Have students keep practicing until they can solve the problems in five seconds or less.

# Mental Math

using _____ to _____ problems in your _____

## Mental Math Strategies

use doubles

use tens

count on or count back

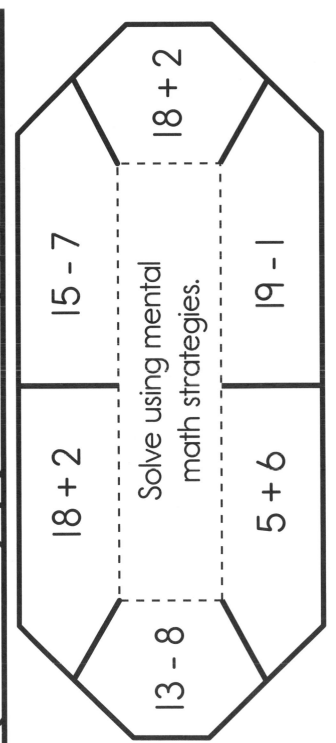

18 + 2

15 − 7

19 − 1

18 + 2

Solve using mental math strategies.

5 + 6

13 − 8

# Even and Odd Numbers

Give each student a handful of linking cubes. Tell students to count out 8 cubes and line them up in equal groups of 2. Ask them if there are any cubes left over from the set of 8. Write the number *8* on the board and label it *even*. Then, ask students to count out 11 cubes and line them up in equal groups of 2. Ask them if there are any cubes left over. Write the number *11* on the board and label it *odd*. Have students count out other numbers on their own and volunteer whether they are odd or even.

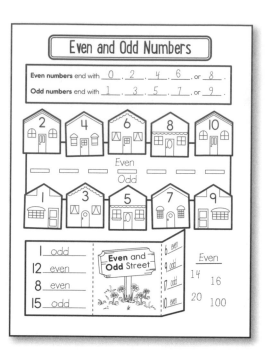

## Creating the Notebook Page

Guide students through the following steps to complete the right-hand page in their notebooks.

1.  Add a Table of Contents entry for the Even and Odd Numbers pages.

2.  Cut out the title and glue it to the top of the page.

3.  Cut out the *Even numbers end with* piece and glue it below the title.

4.  Complete the explanation. (Even numbers end with **0**, **2**, **4**, **6**, or **8**. Odd numbers end with **1**, **3**, **5**, **7**, or **9**.)

5.  Cut out the street and glue it below the *Even numbers end with* piece, leaving enough space to glue houses above it. Write *Even* on the top half of the street and *Odd* on the bottom half.

6.  Cut out the houses. Glue them to the correct sides of the street. Add details such as chimneys, trees, bushes, people, etc., as desired.

7.  Cut out the *Even and Odd Street* flap book. Apply glue to the back of the center section and attach it to the bottom of the page.

8.  In the blank beside each number, write *odd* or *even*. Under the left flap, label the space *Odd*. Write more odd numbers under the flap. Under the right flap, label the space *Even*. Write more even numbers under the flap.

## Reflect on Learning

To complete the left-hand page, have each student draw a chart with numbers from 1 to 20. Ask them to color all of the odd numbers blue and the even numbers yellow. Finally, have each student write a sentence below the chart that describes the pattern of the odd and even numbers, such as *All of the yellow numbers end in 0, 2, 4, 6, or 8.*

# Even and Odd Numbers

**Even numbers** end with _____ , _____ , _____ , _____ , or _____ .

**Odd numbers** end with _____ , _____ , _____ , _____ , or _____ .

1 _____    6 _____

12 _____   9 _____

8 _____    17 _____

15 _____   10 _____

Even and Odd Street

# Arrays

## Introduction

Give each student a handful of linking cubes. Have students make 3 rows of 3 where the rows and columns are equally spaced. Tell students that this pattern is called an *array*. Ask students to count the cubes. Then, ask students to note that there are 3 rows of 3. Ask students to add 3 plus 3, and then add 3 more. Discuss which method was faster and easier. Explain that arrays can make it easier to solve multiplication and division problems. Repeat this process up to 5 rows of 5.

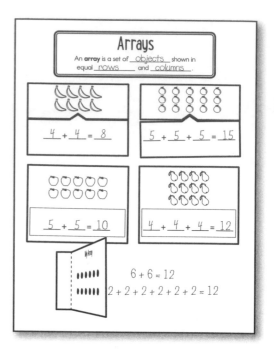

## Creating the Notebook Page

Guide students through the following steps to complete the right-hand page in their notebooks.

1.  Add a Table of Contents entry for the Arrays pages.

2.  Cut out the title and glue it to the top of the page.

3.  Complete the definition of an array. (An array is a set of **objects** shown in equal **rows** and **columns**.)

4.  Cut out the four puzzle pieces. Glue the pieces with arrays below the title. Look at each array and discuss the related addition sentence. Glue the correct puzzle piece below each one. Complete the number sentences (**4 + 4 = 8** and **5 + 5 + 5 = 15**).

5.  Cut out the apples and pears pieces and glue them below the puzzles. Complete the addition sentences (**5 + 5 = 10** and **4 + 4 + 4 = 12**).

6.  Cut out the *My Array* flap. Apply glue to the back of the left section and attach it to the bottom of the page.

7.  Draw an array on top of the flap. Under the flap, write two related addition sentences (rows + rows and columns + columns). Discuss how no matter which way you add, the answers are still the same.

## Reflect on Learning

To complete the left-hand page, have students make their own arrays with up to 25 linking cubes. Students should write two related addition sentences to match each array.

# Arrays

An **array** is a set of _____ shown in equal _____ and _____ .

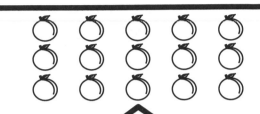

$4 + 4 = 8$

$5 + 5 + 5 = 15$

$5 + 5 = 10$

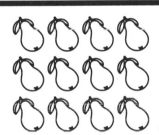

$4 + 4 + 4 = 12$

My Array

# Patterns

## Introduction

Draw a pattern of alternating stars and circles. Ask students to name the shapes aloud, starting at the left and moving right. Ask if they noticed a part that repeats. Explain that this is called a *pattern*. Have a student come to the board and circle the set of objects that repeat. Ask another student to draw the next object in the pattern. Repeat the activity with other patterns. Finally, extend this lesson with patterns that use motions and sound, such as clapping and tapping.

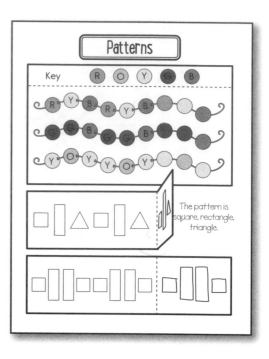

## Creating the Notebook Page

Guide students through the following steps to complete the right-hand page in their notebooks.

1. Add a Table of Contents entry for the Patterns pages.

2. Cut out the title and glue it to the top of the page.

3. Cut out the *Key* flap. Apply glue to the back of the top section and attach it below the title.

4. Color the beads with the correct colors to complete the key in the top section (red, orange, yellow, green, and blue). Then, use the key to color the labeled beads of the first strand of beads. Discuss the pattern and continue it on the unlabeled beads. Repeat the process with all three strands.

5. Under the flap, draw a string of 9 beads. Color the first 6 beads in a pattern. Exchange notebooks with partners. Identify the pattern. Then, use crayons to extend the pattern.

6. Cut out the two shape flaps. Apply glue to the back of the left sections and attach them to the bottom of the page.

7. Identify the pattern on each flap. Then, draw shapes to extend the pattern. Under the flaps, explain the patterns.

## Reflect on Learning

To complete the left-hand page, have students draw several patterns created with objects, shapes, or colors. Have students exchange notebooks with partners and extend each other's patterns.

# Patterns

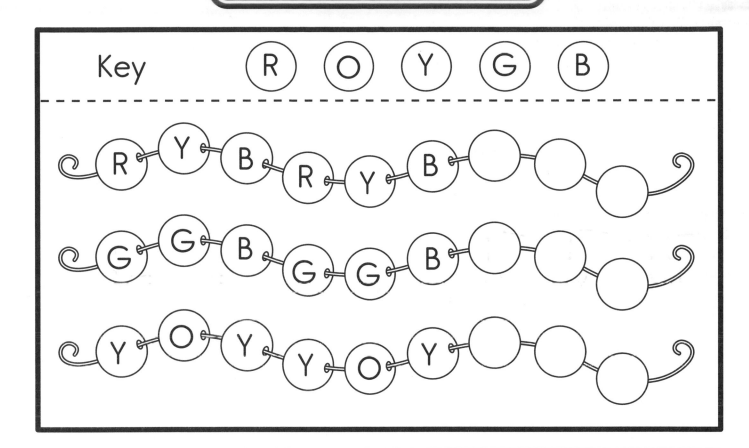

Key: R O Y G B

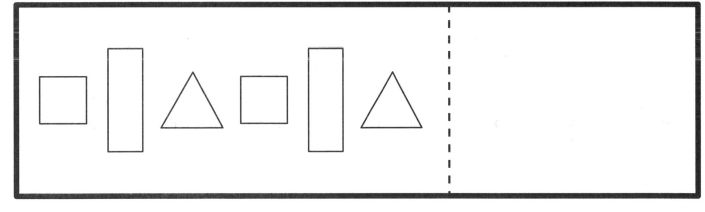

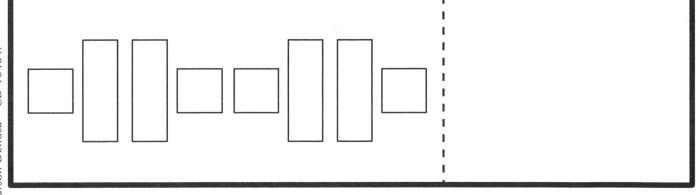

# Skip Counting

## Introduction

Review skip counting by 2s, 5s, and 10s. First, have students count aloud the number of shoes in the class with each student counting his own pair (2, 4, 6, etc.). Then, have students do the same with toes, with each student counting the toes on one foot and then the other (5, 10, 15, etc.). Finally, have students count the number of fingers in the class, with each student counting all of her fingers (10, 20, 30, etc.).

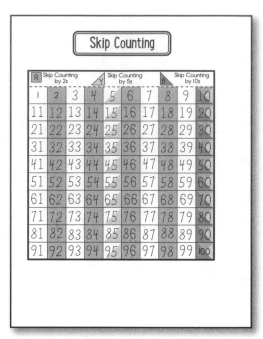

## Creating the Notebook Page

Guide students through the following steps to complete the right-hand page in their notebooks.

1. Add a Table of Contents entry for the Skip Counting pages.

2. Cut out the title and glue it to the top of the page.

3. Cut out the hundred chart. Apply glue to the back of the top section and attach it below the title.

4. Color the key at the top (red, yellow, and blue). Fill in the missing numbers to complete the chart. Then, color the numbers according to the key.

5. Under the flap, write five things observed about the numbers that are the same color and the counting patterns, such as all of the even numbers being red or the 10s being red, yellow, and blue.

## Reflect on Learning

To complete the left-hand page, write a word problem on the board that can be solved by skip counting, such as *There are 7 cars in a parking lot. Each car has 2 headlights. How many total headlights are there?* Or, provide students with copies to glue into their notebooks. Have students solve the problem and explain how they used skip counting to find the answer.

# Skip Counting

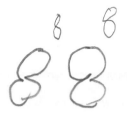

| R  Skip Counting by 2s | | Y  Skip Counting by 5s | | | | B  Skip Counting by 10s | | | |
|----|----|----|----|----|----|----|----|----|----|
| 1  | 2  | 3  | 4  | 5  | 6  | 7  | 8  | 9  | 10 |
| 11 | 12 | 13 | 14 | 15 | 16 | 17 | 18 | 19 | 20 |
| 21 | 22 | 23 | 24 | 25 | 26 | 27 | 28 | 29 | 30 |
| 31 | 32 | 33 | 34 | 35 | 36 | 37 | 38 | 39 | 40 |
| 41 | 42 | 43 | 44 | 45 | 46 | 47 | 48 | 49 | 50 |
| 51 | 52 | 53 | 54 | 55 | 56 | 57 | 58 | 59 | 60 |
| 61 | 62 | 63 | 64 | 65 | 66 | 67 | 68 | 69 | 70 |
| 71 | 72 | 73 | 74 | 75 | 76 | 77 | 78 | 79 | 80 |
| 81 | 82 | 83 | 84 | 85 | 86 | 87 | 88 | 89 | 90 |
| 91 | 92 | 93 | 94 | 95 | 96 | 97 | 98 | 99 | 100 |

# Place Value

Students will need place value mats to complete the introduction activity. To create place value mats, have students make three-column charts labeled Hundreds, Tens, and Ones on small sheets of poster board. Laminate the mats and provide students with write-on/wipe-away markers.

## Introduction

Review place value. Write a three-digit number such as *382* on the board. Ask students to tell you how many ones, how many tens, and how many hundreds are in the number. Then, have them work with partners. Give each pair a die. Have one student roll the die three times, while the other student writes each number on a place value mat in the hundreds, tens, or ones place with a write-on/wipe-away marker. Each time a student writes a number, she must say its value (for example, *3 tens is 30*). The student who rolls the die must read the number correctly once all values have been assigned. Have partners switch roles and repeat the activity.

Place Value

2 hundreds, 200
6 tens, 60
1 one, 1
261

| 348 | 621 |
| ... | 139 |
| 222 | 514 |
| 439 | 842 |

## Creating the Notebook Page

Guide students through the following steps to complete the right-hand page in their notebooks.

1. Add a Table of Contents entry for the Place Value pages.

2. Cut out the title and glue it to the top of the page.

3. Cut out the four rectangular flaps. Apply glue to the back of the left sections and attach them below the title.

4. Look at the base ten blocks. Under each flap, write the number of hundreds, tens, and ones and the value of each (for example, *2 hundreds, 200*). Then, write the numeral.

5. Cut out the shutter fold. Cut on the solid lines to create eight flaps. With the blank side up, fold the flaps toward the center. Apply glue to the gray glue section and attach it to the bottom of the page.

6. Open each flap completely and use the space to draw place value blocks to represent each number. Draw a square to represent a hundreds block, a line to represent a tens rod, and a dot to represent a ones cube.

## Reflect on Learning

To complete the left-hand page, have each student think of a secret number greater than 99. Students should write three or four clues about it such as *It is odd*, *It has 3 tens*, and *It is greater than 218*. Have students say the clues to partners and let their partners ask questions and make guesses. Then, have partners switch roles and repeat the activity.

24

© Carson-Dellosa • CD-104647

# Place Value

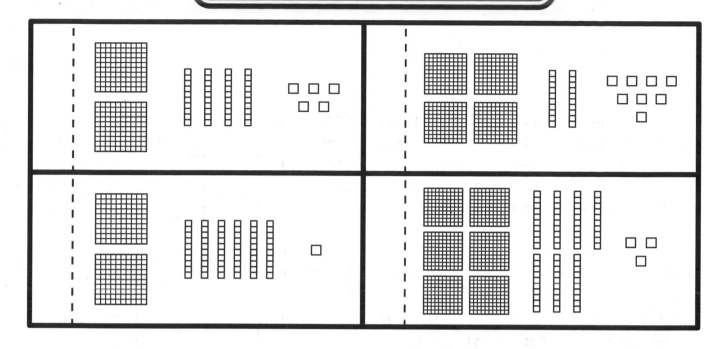

| | | |
|---|---|---|
| 621 | glue | 348 |
| 139 | | 723 |
| 514 | | 222 |
| 842 | | 439 |

# Reading and Writing Numbers

*Students will need base ten blocks to complete the introduction and reflection activities.*

## Introduction

Explain that numbers can be represented and written in different forms. Provide students with base ten blocks. Review and practice the concept of place value by calling out several three-digit numbers for students to represent using base ten blocks. Then, write the number *234* on the board. Ask students to represent the number with the base ten blocks. Then, ask students to write the number in expanded form (200 + 30 + 4) using their base ten blocks as a guide. Finally, have students write the word form for the number 234 (two hundred thirty-four). Repeat the activity with a different three-digit number.

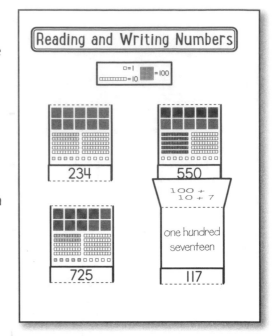

## Creating the Notebook Page

Guide students through the following steps to complete the right-hand page in their notebooks.

1.  Add a Table of Contents entry for the Reading and Writing Numbers pages.

2.  Cut out the title and glue it to the top of the page.

3.  Cut out the base ten blocks key and glue it below the title.

4.  Cut out the trifolds. With the blank sides faceup, fold in the top and bottom sections on the dashed lines so that the small pieces overlap the large pieces. Apply glue to the gray glue sections and attach them to the page.

5.  Look at the number on the bottom flap of each trifold. Color the base ten blocks to represent each number. Open each trifold. On the top section, write the number in expanded form. On the center section, write the number in word form.

## Reflect on Learning

To complete the left-hand page, have students work with partners. Using base ten blocks, students should build three-digit numbers and show them to their partners. Students should write their partners' numbers in standard form, expanded form, and word form in their notebooks. Repeat the activity as time allows.

# Reading and Writing Numbers

| 234 | 550 | 725 |
|---|---|---|
| glue | glue | glue |

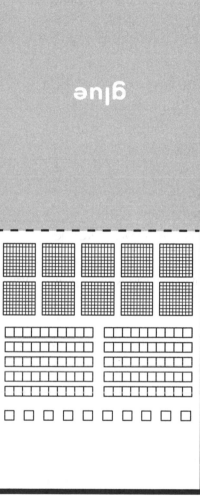

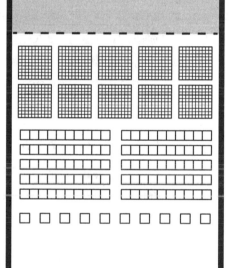

117 | glue

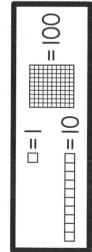

# Comparing and Ordering Numbers

Review the comparison symbols (<, >, and =). Draw a number line on the board from 1 to 10, numbering only the endpoints. Ask a student to write the number *5* in its correct place on the number line. Write two number sentences: *5 < 10* and *10 > 5*. Lay out number tiles from 1 to 10. One at a time, ask students to choose a number, mark it on the number line, and then write a number sentence to compare it with another number on the number line. When students choose the number tiles 1, 5, or 10, students should make number comparisons with the equal sign.

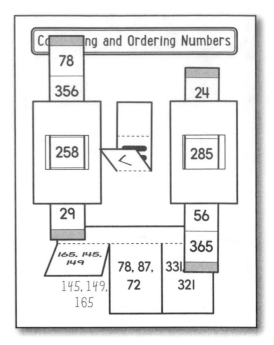

## Creating the Notebook Page

Guide students through the following steps to complete the right-hand page in their notebooks.

1. Add a Table of Contents entry for the Comparing and Ordering Numbers pages.

2. Cut out the title and glue it to the top of the page.

3. Cut out the two blank flap books. Cut on the solid lines to create three flaps on each. Turn each piece facedown. Slide a number strip over the center flap so that one number shows at a time in the center of the blank side. Without removing the number strip, flip over the piece and apply glue to the gray glue sections. Attach it to the left of the page. Repeat the steps with the other flap book and the remaining number strip. Attach it to the right of the page.

4. Cut out the piece with the equal sign. Fold the bottom and top flaps over the equal sign. Apply glue to the back of the middle section. Attach it to the page between the two sliders. Flip down the top flap and draw a greater than symbol (>) on it. Flip up the bottom flap and draw a less than symbol (<) on it.

5. Slide the number strips to make various number comparisons. With each pair of numbers shown, unfold the center flaps to create a true number comparison.

6. Cut out the flap book. Cut on the solid lines to create three flaps. Apply glue to the back of the top section and attach it to the page.

7. Under each flap, write each set of numbers in order from least to greatest.

## Reflect on Learning

To complete the left-hand page, have students write three two- and three-digit numbers in two columns on the left and right sides of the page. Have students exchange notebooks with partners and write comparison symbols to make a true comparison statement for each set of numbers.

# Comparing and Ordering Numbers

glue

glue  glue  glue

glue

glue

glue

glue

==

331, 327, 321

78, 87, 72

165, 145, 149

| 78 | 356 | 110 | 258 | 65 | 29 |
|----|-----|-----|-----|----|-----|
| 24 | 101 | 285 | 92 | 56 | 365 |

# Addition and Subtraction Fluency

*Students will need counters and bingo sheets that contain 25 random two-digit numbers to complete the introduction activity.*

## Introduction

Play addition and subtraction bingo to provide a fun way to develop fluency with math facts. Write one two-digit addition or subtraction problem (no regrouping) on the board to match each answer on the bingo sheets. Play several games with different problems that match the same answers. Finally, discuss with students whether fluency with addition and subtraction facts can make the game easier to play.

## Creating the Notebook Page

Guide students through the following steps to complete the right-hand page in their notebooks.

1. Add a Table of Contents entry for the Addition and Subtraction Fluency pages.

2. Cut out the title and glue it to the top of the page.

3. Cut out the two rectangular flap books. Cut on the solid lines to create six flaps on each. Apply glue to the back of the top sections and attach them below the title.

4. Write the answer to each problem under the flap as quickly and accurately as possible. Notice which math facts you need more practice with.

5. Cut out the eight-flap petal fold. Cut on the solid lines to create eight flaps. Apply glue to the back of the center section and attach it to the page.

6. Write the answer to each problem under the flap.

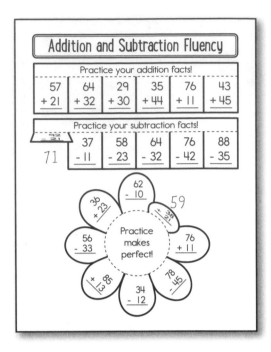

## Reflect on Learning

To complete the left-hand page, have students describe why it is important to be able to quickly and easily add and subtract two-digit numbers. Then, have students reflect on how fluency with two-digit addition and subtraction facts is related to fluency with single-digit addition and subtraction facts.

**30**

# Addition and Subtraction Fluency

## Practice your addition facts!

| 57<br>+ 21 | 64<br>+ 32 | 29<br>+ 30 | 35<br>+ 44 | 76<br>+ 11 | 43<br>+ 45 |
|---|---|---|---|---|---|

## Practice your subtraction facts!

| 92<br>- 21 | 37<br>- 11 | 58<br>- 23 | 64<br>- 32 | 76<br>- 42 | 88<br>- 35 |
|---|---|---|---|---|---|

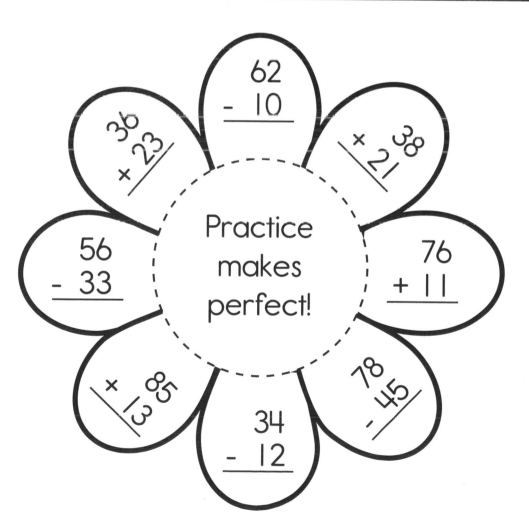

# The Relationship between Addition and Subtraction

## Introduction

Give each student at least 10 counters. Ask students to count out 4 counters and then add 2 more. Ask students to identify how many counters they have in all. Write *4 + 2 = 6*. Now, have students take 2 counters away. Write *6 – 2 = 4* below the addition sentence. Discuss the relationship between addition and subtraction, pointing out that the same three numbers can be used to write four related addition and subtraction sentences. Repeat these steps with other number combinations, including two-digit numbers.

The Relationship between
Addition and Subtraction

If 5 + 4 = 9, then
9 − 4 = 5 .

If 10 − 9 = 1, then
1 + 9 = 10 .

If 3 + 5 = 8, then
8 − 3 = 5 .

4 + 3 = 7
3 + 4 = 7
7 − 4 = 3
7 − 3 = 4

## Creating the Notebook Page

Guide students through the following steps to complete the right-hand page in their notebooks.

1.  Add a Table of Contents entry for The Relationship between Addition and Subtraction pages.

2.  Cut out the title and glue it to the top of the page.

3.  Cut out the three large rectangular pieces and glue them below the title.

4.  Cut out the number blocks. Discuss the inverse nature of addition and subtraction. Glue the numbers in the correct squares to make related number sentences. Stress that the three numbers in the top number sentence will be used for the bottom number sentence, only in a different order.

5.  Cut out the flaps. Apply glue to the back of the top sections and attach them beside each other on the bottom of the page.

6.  Write fact families under each flap using the three numbers on top.

## Reflect on Learning

To complete the left-hand page, have students choose two pairs of two-digit numbers. Under each pair, have them write fact families. Students should write two addition number sentences and two subtraction number sentences under each pair.

| 5 | 4 | 9 | 10 | 9 | 1 | 3 | 5 | 8 |
|---|---|---|---|---|---|---|---|---|

If 5 + 4 = 9, then

9 − 4 = 5 .

If 10 − 9 = 1, then

1 + 9 = 10 .

If 3 + 5 = 8, then

8 − 5 = 3 .

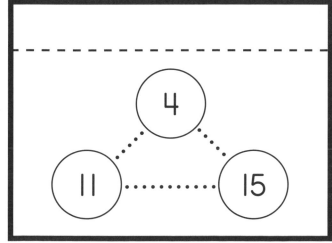

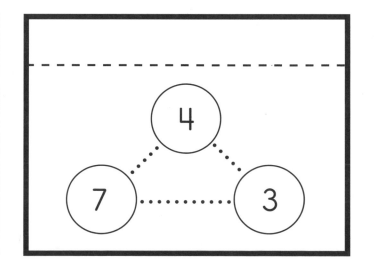

# Finding Missing Addends

## Introduction

Review fact families. Write a plus sign, a minus sign, and an equal sign on index cards. Then, write the numbers from a fact family on separate index cards. Have each student take one index card. Then, have students arrange and rearrange themselves at the front of the class to show each of the four facts in the fact family. Repeat with several different fact families.

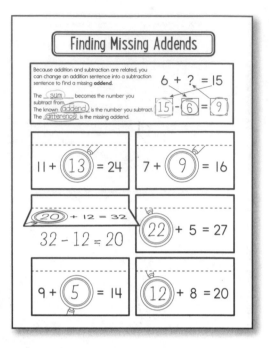

## Creating the Notebook Page

Guide students through the following steps to complete the right-hand page in their notebooks.

1.  Add a Table of Contents entry for the Finding Missing Addends pages.

2.  Cut out the title and glue it to the top of the page.

3.  Cut out the *6 + ? = 15* piece and glue it below the title.

4.  Discuss how addition and subtraction are related. Complete the sentences. (The **sum** becomes the number you subtract from. The known **addend** is the number you subtract. The **difference** is the missing addend.) Then, use the arrows to place the numbers in the correct boxes and complete the related subtraction sentence in the example (**15 – 6 = 9**). Circle each fill-in-the-blank word in a different color and circle the matching part of the example problem in the same color to show the parts of related addition and subtraction sentences.

5.  Cut out the flaps. Apply glue to the back of the top sections and attach them to the page.

6.  Look at the problem on each flap. Write the related subtraction problem under each flap and solve. Then, write the missing addend in the magnifying glass on the flap.

## Reflect on Learning

To complete the left-hand page, write *30 – ? = 23* on the board. Have students reflect on what they learned about missing addends and describe how they would try to find the missing number in a subtraction sentence. Then, have students try to solve for the missing number.

# Finding Missing Addends

Because addition and subtraction are related, you can change an addition sentence into a subtraction sentence to find a missing **addend**.

The _____ becomes the number you subtract from.
The known _____ is the number you subtract.
The _____ is the missing addend.

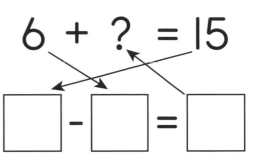

$11 + \bigcirc = 24$

$7 + \bigcirc = 16$

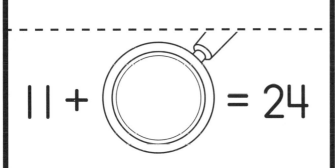

$\bigcirc + 12 = 32$

$\bigcirc + 5 = 27$

$9 + \bigcirc = 14$

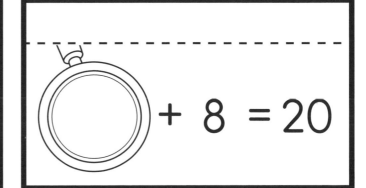

$\bigcirc + 8 = 20$

# Adding More Than Two Addends

## Introduction

Have four students roll two dice each. Use the numbers rolled to create four two-digit numbers. Write the numbers on the board. Have students choose two numbers and add them. Repeat the activity several times.

## Creating the Notebook Page

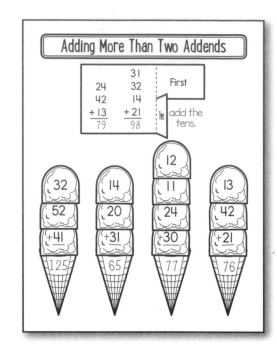

Guide students through the following steps to complete the right-hand page in their notebooks.

1. Add a Table of Contents entry for the Adding More Than Two Addends pages.

2. Cut out the title and glue it to the top of the page.

3. Cut out the *First, Then* piece. Cut on the solid line to create two flaps. Apply glue to the back of the left section and attach it below the title.

4. Under the flaps, write the steps for adding three and four two-digit numbers. (First, **add the ones**. Then, **add the tens**.) Then, solve the example problems by following the steps. If desired, color each flap a different color. Use each color to circle the corresponding step in each example problem.

5. Cut out the ice-cream cones and ice-cream scoops. Glue the ice-cream cones in a row along the bottom of the page.

6. Choose three or four ice-cream scoops to glue on each ice-cream cone. Not all ice-cream scoops may need to be used. Discard any extras. Write a plus sign and a line on each bottom ice-cream scoop. Add the numbers on top of each cone, writing the answer in the blank space on the cone.

## Reflect on Learning

To complete the left-hand page, have students reflect on how adding three and four two-digit numbers is similar to adding two two-digit numbers. Then, students should describe how they would add sets of five and six two-digit numbers.

# Adding More Than Two Addends

```
        31
  24    32      First
  42    14
 +13   +21      Then
```

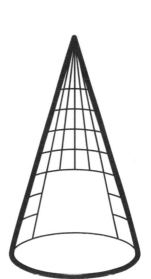

| 41 | 52 | 32 | 33 |

| 14 | 21 | 31 | 20 |

| 30 | 11 | 24 | 12 |

| 13 | 42 | 23 | 22 |

© Carson-Dellosa • CD-104647

# Addition without Regrouping

## Introduction

Review addition within 100. Write a variety of two-digit numbers on index cards. Limit digits to the numerals 0 to 4 so that students will not have to regroup. Give each student an index card. Have students walk around the room while music is playing. When the music stops, have each student turn toward the person closest to him and work together to add their numbers. Repeat several times so that students can practice adding several numbers within 100.

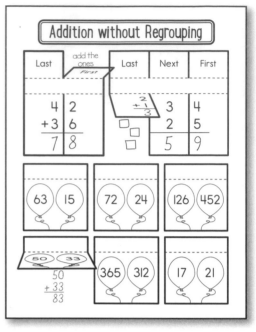

## Creating the Notebook Page

Guide students through the following steps to complete the right-hand page in their notebooks.

1. Add a Table of Contents entry for the Addition without Regrouping pages.

2. Cut out the title and glue it to the top of the page.

3. Cut out the *42 + 36* and *234 + 125* pieces. Cut on the solid lines to create four or six flaps on each piece. Apply glue to the back of the center sections and attach them below the title.

4. Discuss the steps for solving addition problems, including lining up the numbers by place value and always starting with the ones place. Under the top flaps, write the steps for adding. For example, under the *First* flaps, write *add the ones*. Then, follow the steps to solve the example problems on the bottom flaps. Under the flaps, draw base ten blocks to show the addition in each column.

5. Cut out the balloon flaps. Apply glue to the back of the top sections and attach them to the bottom of the page.

6. Rewrite each pair of numbers as an addition problem under each flap, being careful to line up the numbers. Then, solve each problem.

## Reflect on Learning

To complete the left-hand page, write an incorrectly aligned addition problem on the board. Have students copy it into their notebooks and describe what is wrong with the problem. Students should then rewrite the problem correctly and solve it.

# Addition without Regrouping

| Last | First |
|------|-------|
|      |       |

$$\begin{array}{cc} 4 & 2 \\ +3 & 6 \\ \hline \end{array}$$

| Last | Next | First |
|------|------|-------|
|      |      |       |

$$\begin{array}{ccc} 2 & 3 & 4 \\ +1 & 2 & 5 \\ \hline \end{array}$$

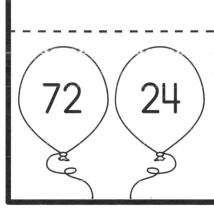

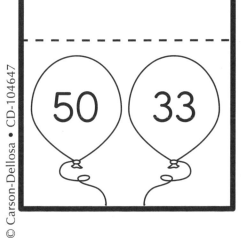

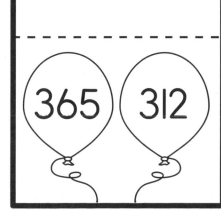

# Addition with Regrouping

*Students will need a sharpened pencil and a paper clip to complete the spinner activity.*

## Introduction

Give students base ten blocks. Write a two-digit addition problem on the board, such as *35 + 24*. Have students model and solve the problem with the base ten blocks. Repeat several times. Then, have students repeat with the problem *25 + 15*. Discuss what students should do with the 10 single ones blocks.

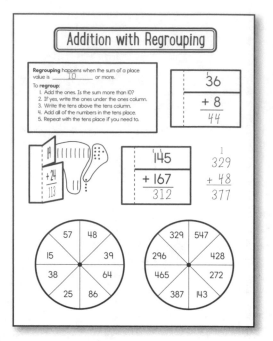

## Creating the Notebook Page

Guide students through the following steps to complete the right-hand page in their notebooks.

1. Add a Table of Contents entry for the Addition with Regrouping pages.

2. Cut out the title and glue it to the top of the page.

3. Cut out the *Regrouping happens* piece and glue it to the left side of the page below the title.

4. Cut out the three addition flap books. Cut on the solid line to create two flaps on each flap book. Apply glue to the back of the left sections. Attach the *36 + 8* flap book to the right side of the page below the title. Attach the two remaining flap books side by side in the middle of the page.

5. Discuss what regrouping is and complete the sentence. (Regrouping happens when the sum of a place value is **10** or more.) Then, discuss the steps.

6. Follow the steps to complete the problems on the flap books. Under each flap, draw the number using base ten notation. Lift both flaps and circle 10 ones to show the regrouping. Then, solve the problem on the flaps.

7. Cut out the spinners and glue them to the bottom of the page.

8. Use a sharpened pencil and a paper clip to create a spinner. Spin the spinner twice to get two numbers and create an addition problem. Write the addition problem on the page beside the flap books and solve. You may choose to spin for two two-digit numbers, two three-digit numbers, or one of each. If desired, create and solve more practice problems on an additional sheet of paper.

## Reflect on Learning

To complete the left-hand page, have students reflect on whether the sum of a place value will ever be 20 or more and explain why or why not.

# Addition with Regrouping

**Regrouping** happens when the sum of a place value is _____ or more.

To **regroup**:
1. Add the ones. Is the sum more than 10?
2. If yes, write the ones under the ones column.
3. Write the tens above the tens column.
4. Add all of the numbers in the tens place.
5. Repeat with the tens place if you need to.

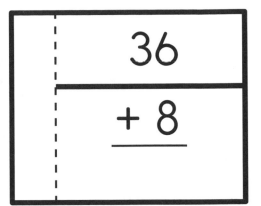

36
+ 8

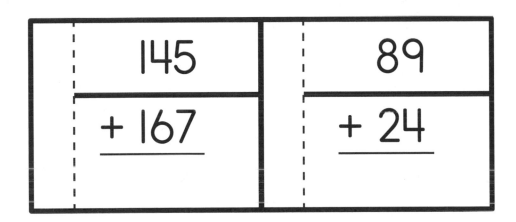

145
+ 167

89
+ 24

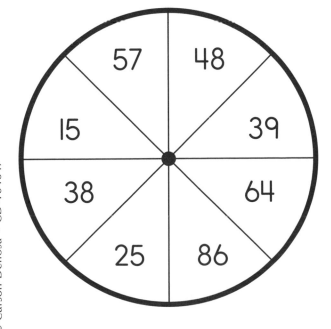

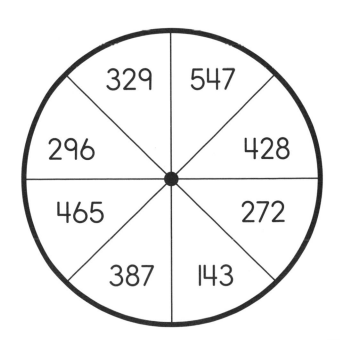

# Subtraction without Regrouping

Students will need base ten blocks and place value mats to complete the introduction activity. To create place value mats, have students make three-column charts labeled Hundreds, Tens, and Ones on small sheets of poster board. Laminate the mats and provide students with write-on/wipe-away markers.

## Introduction

Give students base ten blocks. Write *38 – 16* on the board. Ask students to make 38 (3 tens and 8 ones) on their place value mats. Then, have them take away 16 (1 ten and 6 ones). Emphasize that when subtracting, they will always start on the right with the ones column. Repeat with similar subtraction problems.

## Creating the Notebook Page

Guide students through the following steps to complete the right-hand page in their notebooks.

1. Add a Table of Contents entry for the Subtraction without Regrouping pages.

2. Cut out the title and glue it to the top of the page.

3. Cut out the *65 – 32* and *386 – 265* flap books. Cut on the solid lines to create four or six flaps on each piece. Apply glue to the back of the center sections and attach them below the title.

4. Discuss the steps for solving subtraction problems, including lining up the numbers by place value and always starting with the ones place. Under the top flaps, write the steps for subtracting. For example, under the *First* flaps, write *subtract the ones*. Then, follow the steps to solve the example problems on the bottom flaps. Under the flaps, draw base ten blocks to show the subtraction in each column.

5. Cut out the fish flaps. Apply glue to the back of the top sections and attach them to the bottom of the page.

6. Rewrite each pair of numbers as a subtraction problem under the flap, being careful to line up the numbers. Discuss how the greater number always goes on top. Then, solve each problem.

## Reflect on Learning

To complete the left-hand page, provide students with copies of two subtraction word problems to glue into their notebooks. Ask students to write a subtraction problem for each and solve. Have students explain what steps they used to solve the problems.

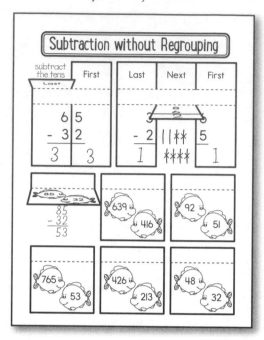

# Subtraction without Regrouping

| Last | First |
|------|-------|
|      |       |

$$
\begin{array}{r} 6\,5 \\ -\ 3\,2 \\ \hline \end{array}
$$

| Last | Next | First |
|------|------|-------|
|      |      |       |

$$
\begin{array}{r} 3\ 8\ 6 \\ -\ 2\ 6\ 5 \\ \hline \end{array}
$$

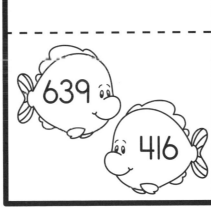

# Subtraction with Regrouping

*Students will need a sharpened pencil and a paper clip to complete the spinner activity.*

## Introduction

Challenge students to explain how regrouping might be used in subtraction. Write *40 – 25* on the board. Discuss how 40 is great enough to subtract 25 from, but you cannot subtract 5 from 0 in the ones column. Introduce the poem *More on top, don't stop./ More on the floor,/Go next door and borrow ten more.* Discuss each line and how it relates to the example problem.

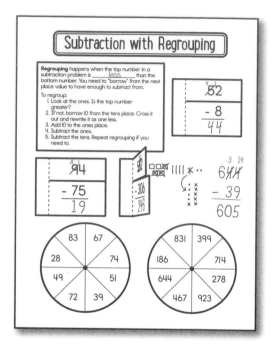

## Creating the Notebook Page

Guide students through the following steps to complete the right-hand page in their notebooks.

1. Add a Table of Contents entry for the Subtraction with Regrouping pages.

2. Cut out the title and glue it to the top of the page.

3. Cut out the *Regrouping happens* piece and glue it to the left side of the page below the title.

4. Cut out the three subtraction flap books. Cut on the solid line to create two flaps on each flap book. Apply glue to the back of the left sections. Attach the *52 – 8* flap book to the right of the *Regrouping happens* piece. Attach the two remaining flap books side by side in the middle of the page.

5. Discuss what regrouping is and complete the sentence. (Regrouping happens when the top number in a subtraction problem is **less** than the bottom number.) Then, discuss the steps.

6. Follow the steps to complete the problems on the flap books. Under each flap, draw the number using base ten notation. Lift both flaps and cross out a ten and redraw it as 10 ones to show the regrouping. Then, solve the problems on the flaps.

7. Cut out the spinners and glue them to the bottom of the page.

8. Use a sharpened pencil and a paper clip to creat a spinner. Spin the spinner twice to get two numbers and create a subtraction problem. Write the subtraction problem on the page beside the flap books and solve. Emphasize how it is important to place the greater number on top. You may choose to spin for two two-digit numbers, two three-digit numbers, or one of each. If desired, create and solve more practice problems on an additional sheet of paper.

## Reflect on Learning

To complete the left-hand page, give students copies of the poem from the introduction to glue into their notebooks. For each line of the poem, have students explain it and provide an example.

**44**

# Subtraction with Regrouping

**Regrouping** happens when the top number in a subtraction problem is _____ than the bottom number. You need to "borrow" from the next place value to have enough to subtract from.

To regroup:
1. Look at the ones. Is the top number greater?
2. If not, borrow 10 from the tens place. Cross it out and rewrite it as one less.
3. Add 10 to the ones place.
4. Subtract the ones.
5. Subtract the tens. Repeat regrouping if you need to.

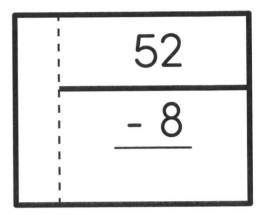

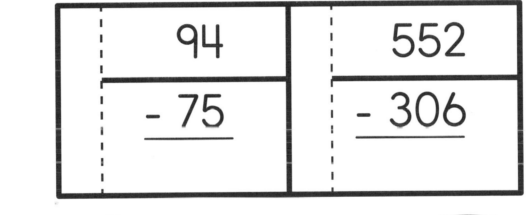

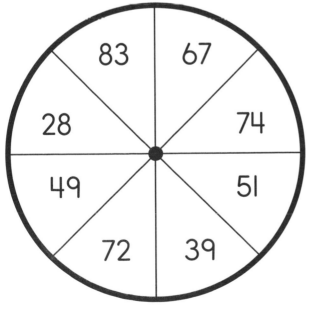

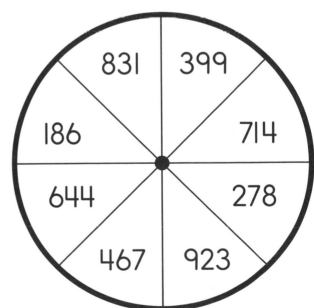

© Carson-Dellosa • CD-104647

# Adding and Subtracting 10 and 100

*Students will need a sharpened pencil and a paper clip to complete the spinner activity.*

## Introduction

Give each student a hundred chart. Say a number such as *57* and challenge students to use the chart to find 10 more or 10 less. Repeat several times with different numbers. As a class, discuss how different students used the chart to quickly find 10 more or 10 less than a number.

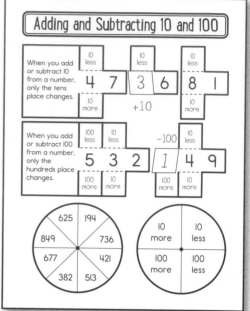

## Creating the Notebook Page

Guide students through the following steps to complete the right-hand page in their notebooks.

1. Add a Table of Contents entry for the Adding and Subtracting 10 and 100 pages.

2. Cut out the title and glue it to the top of the page.

3. Cut out the *47* piece. Cut on the solid lines to create two flaps. Fold the top and bottom flaps over the 4. Apply glue to the back of the left side and the center section on the right and attach it to the top left of the page below the title.

4. Discuss how adding or subtracting 10 changes the place value of a number. With the top flap folded down, write the value that is 10 less on top of the flap (3). Write – *10* on the page under the flap. With the bottom flap up, write the value that is 10 more on top of the flap (5). Write + *10* on the page under the flap. Use the flaps to quickly see how adding and subtracting 10 changes a number.

5. Cut out the *26* and *81* pieces. Apply glue to the back of the center sections and attach them to the page to the right of the *47* piece.

6. Repeat step 4 with the *26* and *81* pieces to complete the top and bottom flaps.

7. Repeat steps 3 and 4 with the *532* and *249* pieces.

8. Cut out the spinners and glue them to the bottom of the page.

9. Use a sharpened pencil and a paper clip to create the number spinner. Spin the spinner. Repeat with the *more/less* spinner. Mentally find the number that is 10 or 100 more or less than the number you landed on. Repeat several times.

## Reflect on Learning

To complete the left-hand page, have students reflect on how to mentally add or subtract 20 or 200 to or from a given number. Students should describe how the number's place value would change.

# Adding and Subtracting 10 and 100

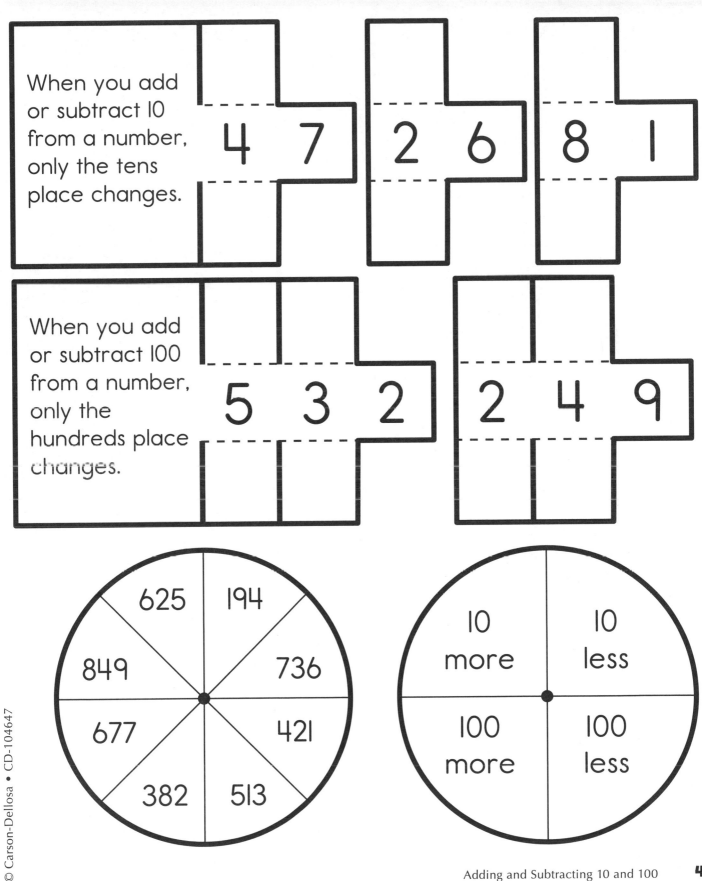

When you add or subtract 10 from a number, only the tens place changes.

4 7    2 6    8 1

When you add or subtract 100 from a number, only the hundreds place changes.

5 3 2    2 4 9

625  194
849        736
677        421
382  513

10 more    10 less
100 more   100 less

# Measurement Tools

Display a ruler, a yardstick, a meterstick, and a measuring tape. Ask students to tell you what they notice about each measuring tool. An answer may be that they all have numbers on them. Review how to measure with each of the tools. Divide students into four teams. Give each team one of the four measuring tools. Have teams measure and record the measurements of different objects in the classroom. As a class, discuss some of the objects each team measured and what difficulties they may have had measuring with their tool. For example, a team may have had difficulty measuring a notebook with a meterstick. Discuss why it is important to choose the correct measuring tool to measure with.

## Creating the Notebook Page

Guide students through the following steps to complete the right-hand page in their notebooks.

1.  Add a Table of Contents entry for the Measurement Tools pages.

2.  Cut out the title and glue it to the top of the page.

3.  Cut out the four pockets. Apply glue to the back of the tabs on each pocket and attach them to the page.

4.  Cut out the picture cards. Look at each card and decide which tool would be best for measuring the object on the card. Sort the cards into the correct pockets. Discuss how some answers may vary and why.

## Reflect on Learning

To complete the left-hand page, have students choose three of the picture cards from the right-hand page. Then, students should write a sentence for each card to explain their reasoning for determining which pocket to place the object in.

# Measurement Tools

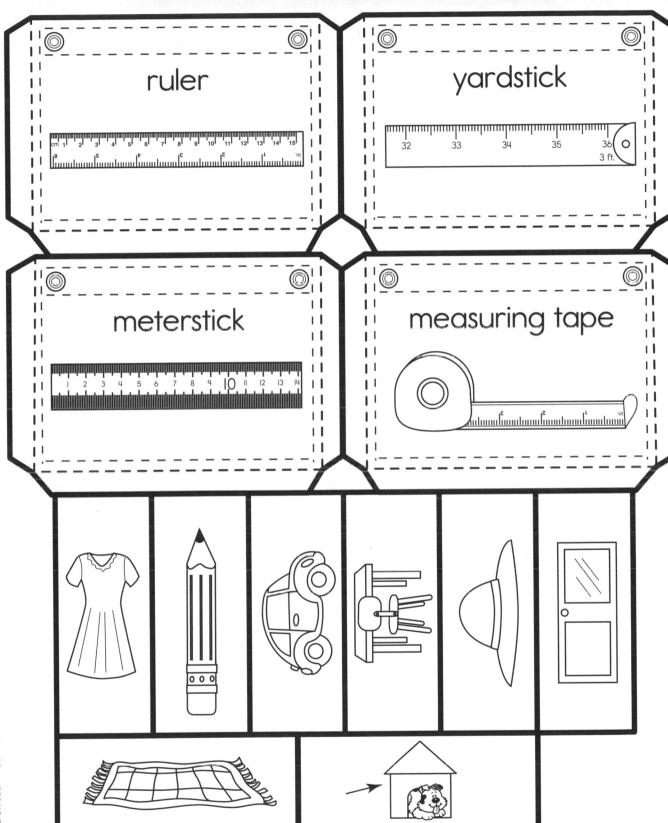

ruler

yardstick

32  33  34  35  36
3 ft.

meterstick

1  2  3  4  5  6  7  8  9  10  11  12  13  14

measuring tape

# Measuring Length

## Introduction

Review measurement. Give each student a sheet of paper. Ask students to estimate the length of items that are less than 12 inches, including their hands, shoes, books, or other items in the classroom. Have students make lists of the items and record their estimates on their papers. Then, give each student a ruler. Ask students to measure each item and write the actual lengths beside their estimates.

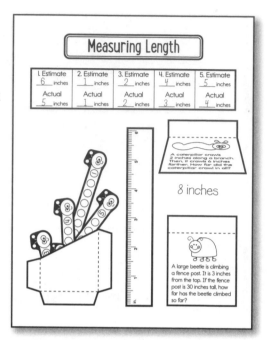

## Creating the Notebook Page

Guide students through the following steps to complete the right-hand page in their notebooks.

1. Add a Table of Contents entry for the Measuring Length pages.

2. Cut out the title and glue it to the top of the page.

3. Cut out the *Estimate* piece and glue it below the title.

4. Cut out the pocket. Apply glue to the back of the tabs and attach it to the bottom left of the page.

5. Cut out the ruler and attach it vertically beside the pocket.

6. Cut out the caterpillars. When not in use, store them in the pocket. (Note: Worm 1 may need to be folded to fit better.)

7. Lay the caterpillars side by side. Estimate the length of each and write it in the correct box on the *Estimate* strip. Review how to measure, starting at the bottom of the ruler. Then, measure each caterpillar and record the actual measurement.

8. Cut out the two flaps. Apply glue to the back of the top sections and attach them to the right side of the page.

9. Read the problem on each flap. Solve the problem under the flap.

## Reflect on Learning

To complete the left-hand page, have students write about the results on their *Estimate* pieces. Ask them to explain the differences between their estimates and the actual lengths, including any patterns they see and why these occurred. Students who estimated correctly may also explain how they are able to make such good "guesses."

# Measuring Length

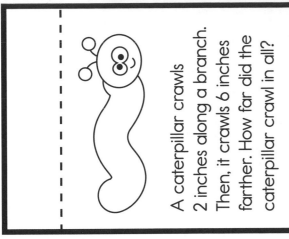

A caterpillar crawls 2 inches along a branch. Then, it crawls 6 inches farther. How far did the caterpillar crawl in all?

A large beetle is climbing a fence post. It is 3 inches from the top. If the fence post is 30 inches tall, how far has the beetle climbed so far?

in. 1 2 3 4 5 6

| 1. Estimate | 2. Estimate | 3. Estimate | 4. Estimate | 5. Estimate |
|---|---|---|---|---|
| _____ inches | _____ inches | _____ inches | _____ inches | _____ inches |
| Actual | Actual | Actual | Actual | Actual |
| _____ inches | _____ inches | _____ inches | _____ inches | _____ inches |

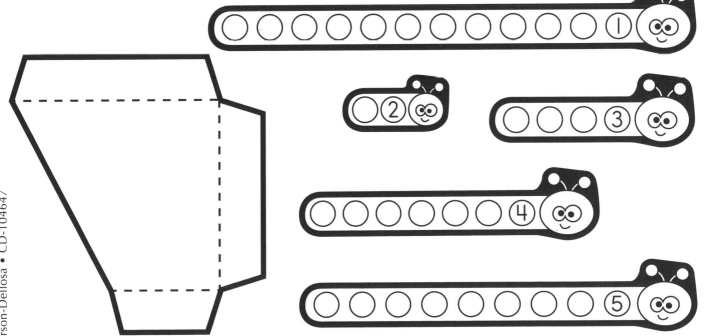

# Comparing Lengths

## Introduction

Before the lesson, cut various lengths of ribbon up to 6 inches long in whole-inch increments. Give each student a ruler with inches and centimeters. Ask students what they notice about the ruler. Write their observations on the board. Discuss the inch and centimeter sides of a ruler. Give each student a length of ribbon. Have students measure their pieces of ribbon in inches. Then, have students place themselves into six groups according to the lengths of their ribbons. Students should compare the lengths of their ribbons to verify they are in the correct groups.

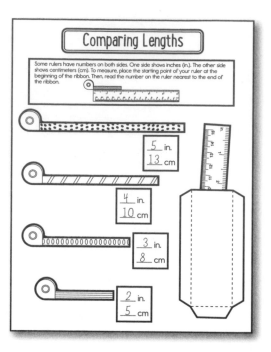

## Creating the Notebook Page

Guide students through the following steps to complete the right-hand page in their notebooks.

1.  Add a Table of Contents entry for the Comparing Lengths pages.

2.  Cut out the title and glue it to the top of the page.

3.  Cut out the pocket. Apply glue to the back of the tabs and attach the pocket to the bottom right of the page.

4.  Cut out the *Some rulers have* piece and glue it below the title. Discuss how to determine the different sides of a ruler and how to use a ruler to measure an object.

5.  Cut out the ruler piece. Store the ruler in the pocket when not in use.

6.  Cut out the ribbon pieces and the four *in./cm* pieces. Glue the ribbon pieces and *in./cm* pieces along the left side of the page.

7.  Use the ruler to measure each ribbon in inches and write the answer. Then, measure the ribbon in centimeters and write the answer. Discuss how to round to the nearest whole centimeter if necessary.

## Reflect on Learning

To complete the left-hand page, return the lengths of ribbon used in the introduction activity. Have students measure the ribbons in inches and centimeters and write each measurement in their notebooks. Then, have students compare the two measurements and answer the following prompt: *Why is it important to know what unit of measurement you are measuring with?*

# Comparing Lengths

Some rulers have numbers on both sides. One side shows inches (in.). The other side shows centimeters (cm). To measure, place the starting point of your ruler at the beginning of the ribbon. Then, read the number on the ruler nearest to the end of the ribbon.

_____ in.

_____ cm

_____ in.

_____ cm

_____ in.

_____ cm

_____ in.

_____ cm

Comparing Lengths  **53**

# Whole Numbers on a Number Line

## Introduction

Review number lines. Draw three number lines with six tick marks on each one. Label the first and last points on each one as follows: 0 and 5 on the first number line, 0 and 25 on the second number line, 0 and 50 on the third number line. Have volunteers come to the board and fill in the missing numbers on the first number line. Discuss how this number line counts by 1s. Ask students if the second number line student counts by 1s. Discuss why it does not. Have volunteers come to the board to complete the second number line. Discuss how the number line counts by 5s. Extend the number line and allow volunteers to fill in the additional numbers. Repeat the activity with the third number line.

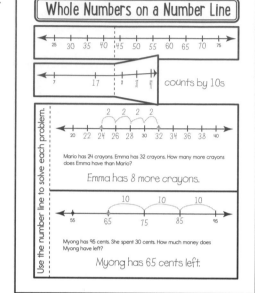

## Creating the Notebook Page

Guide students through the following steps to complete the right-hand page in their notebooks.

1.  Add a Table of Contents entry for the Whole Numbers on a Number Line pages.

2.  Cut out the title and glue it to the top of the page.

3.  Cut out the two number line flaps. Apply glue to the back of the left sections and attach them below the title.

4.  Study each number line and fill in the missing numbers. Under each flap describe how you determined the missing numbers. (The number line that starts with 25 counts by 5s. The number line that starts with 7 counts by 10s.)

5.  Cut out the flap book. Cut on the solid line to create two flaps. Apply glue to the back of the left section and attach it to the page.

6.  Complete the number line on the top flap. Read the word problem. Use the number line to help you solve the problem. Write the answer on the flap. Under the flap, explain how you used the number line to help you solve the problem.

7.  Repeat step 6 with the bottom flap.

## Reflect on Learning

To complete the left-hand page, have students draw two number lines with start points and end points based on a counting pattern such as counting by 5s. Number the first and last points but not the ticks in between. Then, divide students into pairs. Have students trade notebooks and label each tick on their partners' number lines.

# Whole Numbers on a Number Line

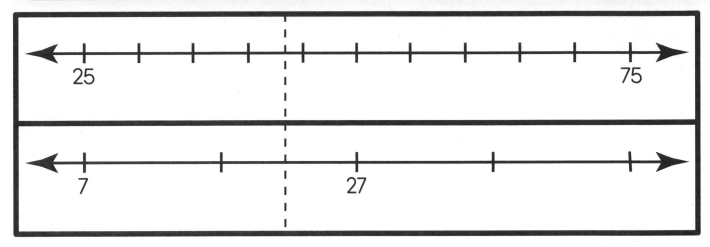

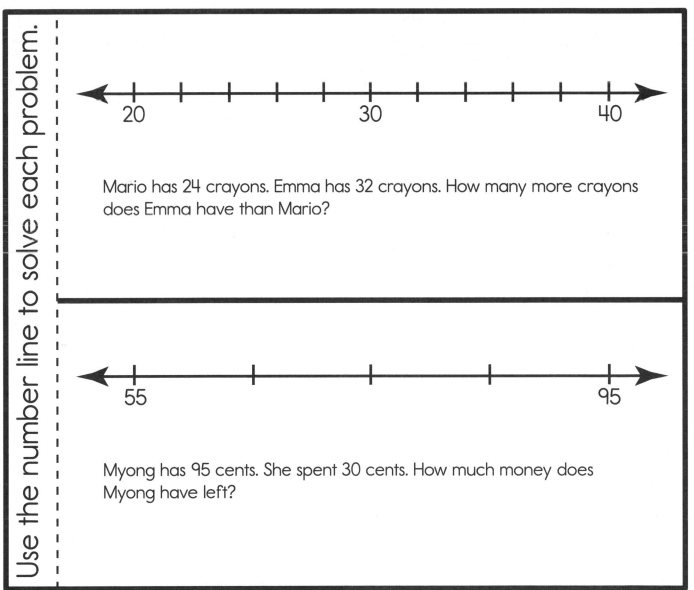

Mario has 24 crayons. Emma has 32 crayons. How many more crayons does Emma have than Mario?

Myong has 95 cents. She spent 30 cents. How much money does Myong have left?

Use the number line to solve each problem.

# Time

*Students will need a brass paper fastener to complete this activity.*

## Introduction

Review time to the hour and half hour. Give each student a small paper plate and a bendy straw. Have each student write numbers on the paper plate to make it look like a clock face and bend the straw so that the short end becomes the hour hand and the long end becomes the minute hand. (Students may need to cut some length off of the long end.) Say times such as *10:00, 5:30,* and *1:30.* Each student should model the times on her clock by moving the straw to the correct position on the clock face. Repeat with several different times.

## Creating the Notebook Page

Guide students through the following steps to complete the right-hand page in their notebooks.

1. Add a Table of Contents entry for the Time pages.

2. Cut out the title and glue it to the top of the page.

3. Cut out the clock face and the clock hands. Push a brass paper fastener through the center dots of the pieces to attach them. It may be helpful to create the hole in each piece separately first. Apply glue to the back of the clock and attach it to the center of the page with the 60 at the top. The brass paper fastener should not go through the page, and the hands should spin freely.

4. Cut out the flaps. Apply glue to the back of the narrow section of each flap and attach the flaps to the page around the clock face so that a flap is where each number should be.

5. On the flaps, write the numbers to complete the clock face. Under each flap, write the number of minutes the position represents. For example, under the 3, you should write *15.*

6. Discuss how to tell and write time to the nearest five minutes. Say times to the nearest five minutes and move the hands to model the times. Then, model times with the hands and write the related times on the page.

## Reflect on Learning

To complete the left-hand page, have students draw analog clocks to show the different times in their daily schedule, such as when school starts; start times for lunch, specials, or recess; or when school ends. If necessary, round times to the nearest five minutes.

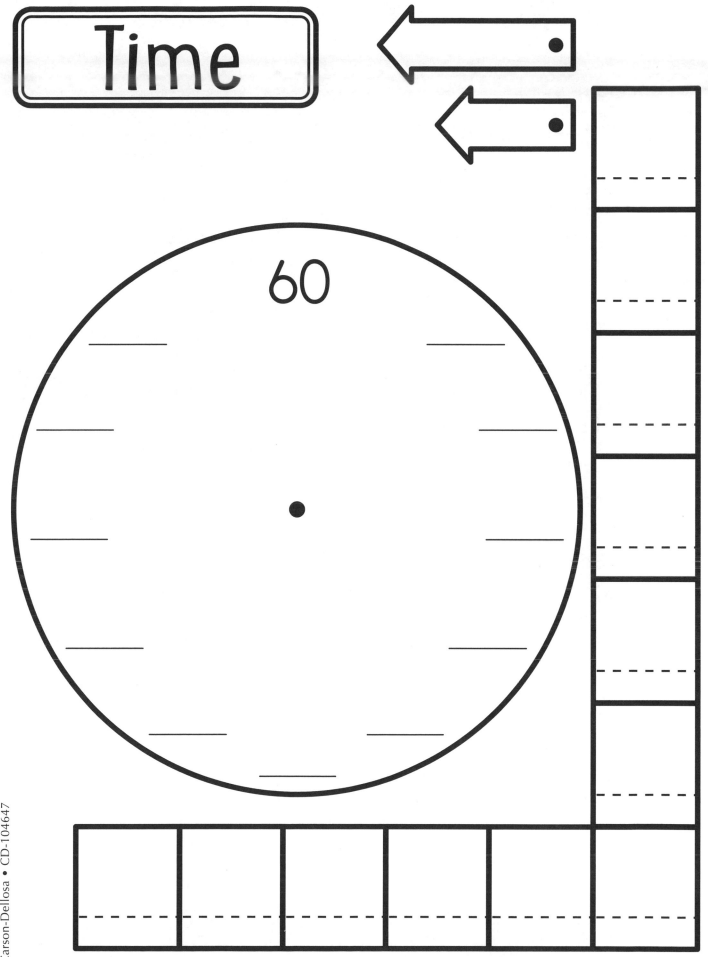

# Time

60

# Pennies, Nickels, and Dimes

**Introduction**

Divide students into small groups. Give each group a blank poster board with the word *money* written in the center. Challenge groups to write and draw everything they know about money on the poster board to create a mind map about money. Allow groups to share their posters and discuss what money is and is not.

**Creating the Notebook Page**

Guide students through the following steps to complete the right-hand page in their notebooks.

1. Add a Table of Contents entry for the Pennies, Nickels, and Dimes pages.

2. Cut out the title and glue it to the top of the page.

3. Cut out the flap book. Cut on the solid lines to create three flaps. Apply glue to the back of the top section and attach it to the page below the title.

4. Cut out the coins.

5. Look at the front and back of each coin and discuss the distinguishing characteristics. Glue each coin to the top of the correct flap on the flap book. Under the flap, write the value of each coin with the numeral and cent symbol as well as in word form.

6. Cut out the toy flaps. Apply glue to the back of the top sections and attach them to the bottom of the page.

7. Look at the value of the toy on each flap. Under the flap, draw the coins it would take to buy the toy. To draw each coin, draw a circle and write *1¢*, *5¢*, or *10¢* in the center.

**Reflect on Learning**

To complete the left-hand page, assign a value from 1¢ to 5¢ to each letter of the alphabet. If desired, provide each student with a key to glue in his notebook. Have students find the value of their names. Then, students should draw that value in pennies, nickels, and dimes.

# Pennies, Nickels, and Dimes

| penny | nickel | dime |
|-------|--------|------|
|       |        |      |

Action Figure 40¢

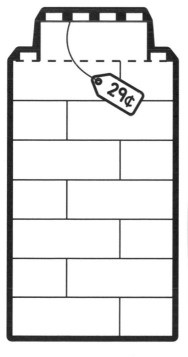

29¢

32¢

# Quarters, Half-Dollars, and Dollars

*This lesson is designed so that half-dollars can be easily removed. If they are not being taught, discard the flap and coin front and back.*

## Introduction

Review pennies, nickels, and dimes. Display large copies of each coin. As a class, identify and name each coin. Then, practice counting coins to find the total. Discuss the similarities and differences between the coins. Ask students to imagine an item that costs 98¢. How many pennies would that be? How many nickels? How many dimes? Explain that coins that are worth more money, such as quarters and half-dollars, make it easier to form greater amounts of money. The same is true of paper money.

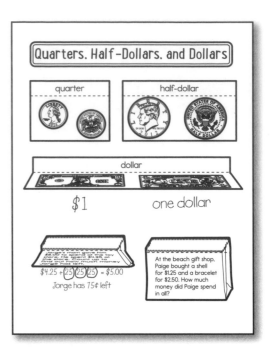

## Creating the Notebook Page

Guide students through the following steps to complete the right-hand page in their notebooks.

1.  Add a Table of Contents entry for the Quarters, Half-Dollars, and Dollars pages.

2.  Cut out the title and glue it to the top of the page.

3.  Cut out the flaps. Apply glue to the back of the top sections and attach them to the page below the title.

4.  Cut out the coins and bills.

5.  Look at the front and back of each coin and bill and discuss their distinguishing characteristics. Glue each coin or bill to the top of the correct flap. Under each flap, write the value of the coin or bill with the numeral and cent or dollar symbol as well as the word form.

6.  Cut out the paper bag flaps. Apply glue to the back of the top sections and attach them to the bottom of the page.

7.  Read the problem on each flap. Solve the problem under the flap.

## Reflect on Learning

To complete the left-hand page, display an ad from a local store. Have students choose three items and draw the coins or bills it would take to buy each item.

# Quarters, Half-Dollars, and Dollars

| quarter | half-dollar |
|---|---|
|  |  |

| dollar |
|---|
|  |

Jorge's mom gave him $5.00 to spend at the toy store. He spent $4.25 at the store. Count up to find out how much money Jorge has left.

At the beach gift shop, Paige bought a shell for $1.25 and a bracelet for $2.50. How much money did Paige spend in all?

# Picture Graphs

## Introduction

Review the different types of graphs the class has studied. Draw an example of each graph on the board. Then, have students label the graphs with the correct names. Discuss the parts of each graph. As a class, discuss how the graphs are the same and how the graphs are different.

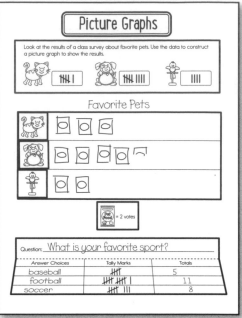

## Creating the Notebook Page

Guide students through the following steps to complete the right-hand page in their notebooks.

1. Add a Table of Contents entry for the Picture Graphs pages.

2. Cut out the title and glue it to the top of the page.

3. Cut out the tally marks piece and glue it below the title.

4. Cut out the blank picture graph, the three picture labels, and the scale piece. Glue the picture graph below the tally mark piece, leaving space above to write a title. Glue the scale piece below the picture graph. Glue the label pieces on the left side of the picture graph.

5. Discuss what picture graphs are and look at the data on the tally mark piece. Use the data and the scale to complete the picture graph. Decide on a title and write it above the graph. Discuss how to show data when the scale doesn't match (for example, how to show an odd number when the scale represents data by 2s).

6. Cut out the *Question* flap. Apply glue to the back of the top section and attach it to the bottom of the page.

7. Decide on a survey question and write it in the space provided. Write possible answers in the left side of the chart. Ask several people the survey question and write their answers in the center column of the chart using tally marks. Write the totals in the right-hand column. Use the data to draw a picture graph under the flap.

## Reflect on Learning

To complete the left-hand page, explain to students that the scale of a picture graph can be changed. Have students reconstruct the Favorite Pets pictograph from the right-hand page using a scale of 1 instead of 2. Each student should write a sentence or two to compare the two graphs.

# Picture Graphs

Look at the results of a class survey about favorite pets. Use the data to construct a picture graph to show the results.

  | MMM I

 | MMM IIII

| IIII

     = 2 votes

Question: _____

| Answer Choices | Tally Marks | Totals |
|----------------|-------------|--------|
|                |             |        |
|                |             |        |
|                |             |        |

# Bar Graphs

## Introduction

Have students answer a survey question such as *What is your favorite color?* or *What time do you go to bed?* List the answers on the board. Have students look at the list and ask them questions such as *What is the most popular color?*, *What is the least popular color?*, etc. As a class, discuss if it was easy or difficult to answer the questions with the way the data was shown and why. Explain that bar graphs can be used to make data easier to understand.

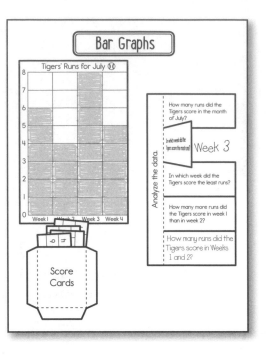

## Creating the Notebook Page

Guide students through the following steps to complete the right-hand page in their notebooks.

1. Add a Table of Contents entry for the Bar Graphs pages.

2. Cut out the title and glue it to the top of the page.

3. Cut out the *Score Cards* pocket. Apply glue to the back of the tabs and attach it to the bottom of the page.

4. Cut out the score cards and store them in the *Score Cards* pocket.

5. Cut out the graph and glue it to the left side of the page below the title.

6. Use the information on the score cards to complete the bar graph.

7. Cut out the flap book. Cut on the solid lines to create five flaps. Apply glue to the back of the left section and attach it to the right side of the page.

8. Read the questions. Use the bar graph to answer each question. Write the answer under the flap. On the last flap, write your own question. Exchange notebooks with a partner and answer each other's questions.

## Reflect on Learning

To complete the left-hand page, have each student use the data from the introduction to create a bar graph. Each student should write and answer two questions about the bar graph.

# Bar Graphs

## Score Cards

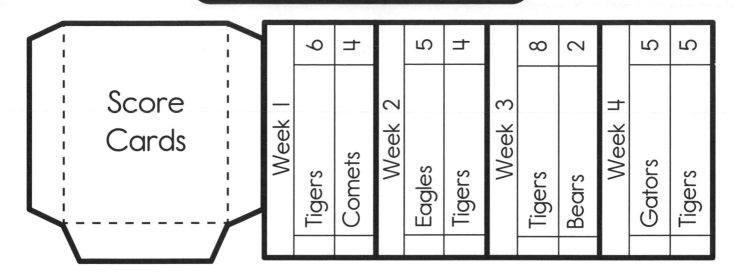

| Week 1 | | Week 2 | | Week 3 | | Week 4 | |
|---|---|---|---|---|---|---|---|
| Tigers | 6 | Eagles | 5 | Tigers | 8 | Gators | 5 |
| Comets | 4 | Tigers | 4 | Bears | 2 | Tigers | 5 |

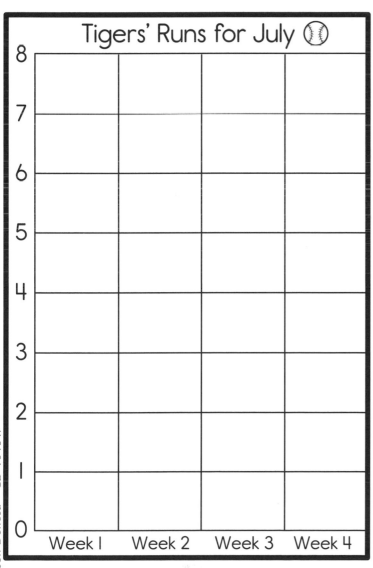

Tigers' Runs for July

8
7
6
5
4
3
2
1
0

Week 1    Week 2    Week 3    Week 4

## Analyze the data.

How many runs did the Tigers score in the month of July?

In which week did the Tigers score the most runs?

In which week did the Tigers score the least runs?

How many more runs did the Tigers score in week 1 than in week 2?

# Line Plots

## Introduction

Give each student a self-stick note. Have each student draw a large *X* on his self-stick note. Then, ask a survey question such as *How many books are in your desk?* or *How many teeth have you lost?* Draw the axes of a bar graph on the board and have students place their self-stick notes above the appropriate columns to answer the question and complete the bar graph. Discuss the features of a bar graph such as the bars, title, axes, and scale. Then, erase the *y*-axis and change the *x*-axis to a number line so that the graph looks like a line plot. Explain that line plots are similar to bar graphs and show numerical data.

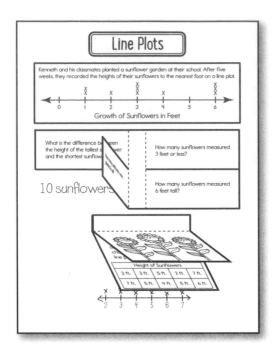

## Creating the Notebook Page

Guide students through the following steps to complete the right-hand page in their notebooks.

1. Add a Table of Contents entry for the Line Plots pages.

2. Cut out the title and glue it to the top of the page.

3. Cut out the line plot piece and glue it below the title.

4. Discuss the parts of a line plot and how data is recorded on a line plot.

5. Cut out the flap book. Cut on the solid lines to create four flaps. Apply glue to the back of the center section and attach it below the line plot.

6. Read the question on each flap. Use the line plot to answer the question and write the answer under the flap.

7. Cut out the two flaps. Apply glue to the gray glue section and place the sunflower flap on top to create a two-flap book. Apply glue to the back of the top section and attach it to the bottom of the page.

8. Read the problem and look at the data. Use the data to construct a line plot under the bottom flap.

## Reflect on Learning

To complete the left-hand page, have students measure the lengths of objects in their desks to the nearest inch, recording the data in their notebooks. Then, students should use the data to create line plots.

# Line Plots

Kenneth and his classmates planted a sunflower garden at their school. After five weeks, they recorded the heights of their sunflowers to the nearest foot on a line plot.

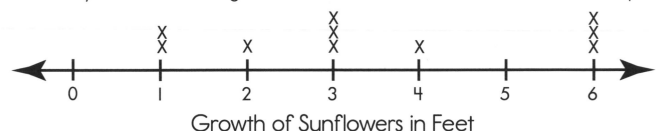

Growth of Sunflowers in Feet

What is the difference between the height of the tallest sunflower and the shortest sunflower?

How many sunflowers measured 3 feet or less?

How many sunflowers were planted in all?

How many sunflowers measured 6 feet tall?

glue

Kenneth and his classmates measured the sunflowers again after two weeks. They made a chart to show the data. Construct a line plot to show the new data.

| Height of Sunflowers | | | | |
|---|---|---|---|---|
| 3 ft. | 3 ft. | 5 ft. | 2 ft. | 7 ft. |
| 7 ft. | 5 ft. | 4 ft. | 5 ft. | 6 ft. |

# Identifying Polygons

## Introduction

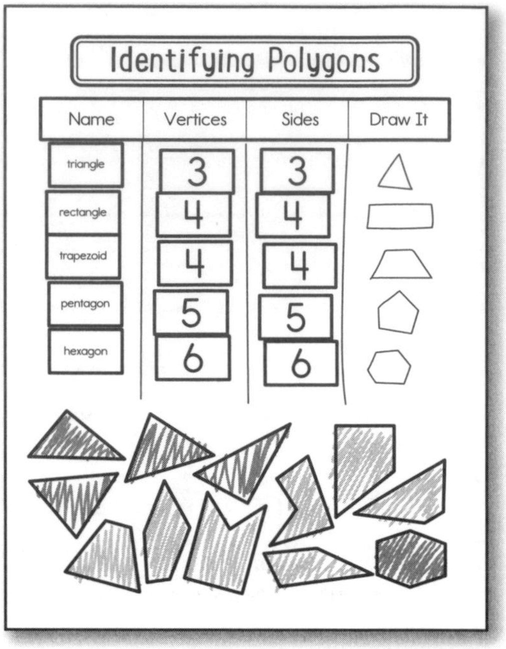

Draw a circle, a square, a heart, a pentagon, and a triangle on the board. Explain that polygons are closed, straight-sided plane figures. Explain that a polygon with three sides is called a *triangle,* a polygon with four sides is called a *quadrilateral,* and a polygon with five sides is called a *pentagon.* Then, have a volunteer come to the board and circle the three polygons. Ask him to explain his choices. Next, give each student a self-stick note with either a polygon or a non-polygon shape drawn on it. Draw two circles on the board. Label the circles *Polygon* and *Not a Polygon.* Have students bring their self-stick notes to the board and place them in the correct circles. Discuss how students knew which circles to place their shapes in.

## Creating the Notebook Page

Guide students through the following steps to complete the right-hand page in their notebooks.

1. Add a Table of Contents entry for the Identifying Polygons pages.

2. Cut out the title and glue it to the top of the page.

3. Cut out the *Name/Vertices* piece and glue it below the title. Continue the lines down from the *Name/Vertices* piece to form a four-column chart below the title.

4. Cut out the 15 shape name and number cards. Glue the shape names in the first column. Think about the attributes of the shapes on the remaining cards. Then, sort and glue the cards under the correct headings.

5. In the *Draw It* column, use the attributes to help you draw each shape.

6. Cut out the polygons and glue them to the bottom of the page. Use the following color code to color the polygons: triangles–red; quadrilaterals–green; pentagons–blue; hexagons–yellow. Then, use the code to color the shape name cards in the first column of the chart.

## Reflect on Learning

To complete the left-hand page, have each student draw a polygon superhero using polygons from the right-hand page. Have students label the polygons used.

# Identifying Polygons

| Name | Vertices | Sides | Draw It |
|---|---|---|---|
| 6 | 6 | trapezoid | 3 | triangle |
| hexagon | 4 | 4 | 4 | 3 |
| 5 | 5 | rectangle | 4 | pentagon |

# Identifying Solid Shapes

## Introduction

Review the difference between 2-D and 3-D shapes. As a class, think of a hand signal to represent flat shapes, such as a hand held out flat; and a hand signal to represent solid shapes, such as a fist. Say different shapes such as *square, sphere, triangle, cone, cube,* etc. Students should make the correct hand signal for each shape to show that it is a 2-D, or flat shape; or a 3-D, or solid shape.

## Creating the Notebook Page

Guide students through the following steps to complete the right-hand page in their notebooks.

1. Add a Table of Contents entry for the Identifying Solid Shapes pages.

2. Cut out the title and glue it to the top of the page.

3. Cut out the *3-D Shapes* piece and glue it below the title.

4. Read and complete the poem. (3-D shapes are fat, not **flat**. A **cone** is like a party hat. A **prism** is like a building tall. A **sphere** is like a bouncy ball. A **cylinder** is like a can of pop. A **cube** is like a die you drop.) Draw a line to match each line of the poem to the correct picture.

5. Cut out the *Cube* piece. Apply glue to the back of the *Cube* section and attach it to the bottom of the page.

6. Under each flap, complete the category on top. So, under the *Vertices* flap, write the total number of vertices on a cube. Use a different color to highlight the edges, faces, and vertices of the shape. Fold on the dashed lines to model a 3-D cube.

7. On the page around the cube, write additional real-world examples of cubes.

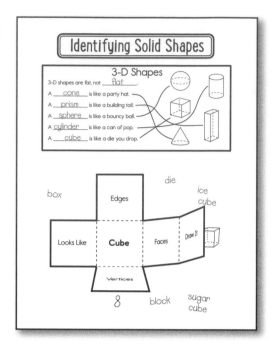

## Reflect on Learning

To complete the left-hand page, have each student choose a shape from the *3-D Shapes* piece on the right-hand page. Each student should write the name of the shape at the top of the page. Next, have students draw the shape. Below the shapes, have students write the number of edges, faces, and vertices. Finally, students should write at least two real world examples of the shapes. It may be helpful to provide students with geometric shape manipulatives to complete this activity.

# Identifying Solid Shapes

## 3-D Shapes

3-D shapes are fat, not _____.

A _____ is like a party hat.

A _____ is like a building tall.

A _____ is like a bouncy ball.

A _____ is like a can of pop.

A _____ is like a die you drop.

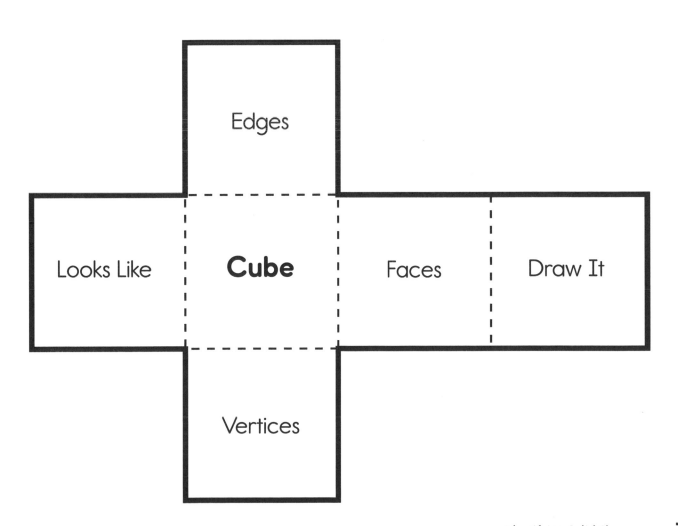

Edges

Looks Like | **Cube** | Faces | Draw It

Vertices

# Partitioning Rectangles

## Introduction

Introduce the word *partition*, explaining that it means to divide something into equal parts. Give students blank sheets of paper. Direct them to fold the papers in half horizontally and then open them again. Have them draw lines along the folds. Discuss how many equal parts the sheets of paper have been folded into. Ask students if they know the names for the equal parts (halves). Have students fold the sheets of paper in half again as before and then fold them in half again. When students open their sheets of paper, they will see four equal parts. Have them draw lines along the new folds. Ask students if they know the name for the equal parts (fourths).

**Partitioning Rectangles**

You can **partition** rectangles into equal parts using rows and columns. This rectangle has 3 rows and 3 columns, which creates 9 equal parts.

## Creating the Notebook Page

Guide students through the following steps to complete the right-hand page in their notebooks.

1. Add a Table of Contents entry for the Partitioning Rectangles pages.

2. Cut out the title and glue it to the top of the page.

3. Cut out the *You can partition* piece and glue it below the title.

4. Count the number of equal parts. Discuss how the rectangle was partitioned.

5. Cut out each of the six "quilt" pieces. Glue them together on the page so that their edges touch to create a quilt.

6. Trace the dotted lines on four of the quilt pieces to partition them into equal parts. Draw lines on the two remaining pieces to partition them into equal parts of your choosing. Use crayons or markers to create a colorful quilt partitioned into equal shapes.

## Reflect on Learning

To complete the left-hand page, have students draw three rectangles. Each rectangle should be the same size. Ask them to use a different way to divide each rectangle into four equal parts. Then, have them shade one section in each. Finally, students should write short paragraphs to describe what is the same (each is a rectangle divided into four equal parts) and what is different (the shape of the parts). Have students explain how this proves that the shape of each partition doesn't matter as long as the entire shape is divided equally. For example, a rectangle may be divided into four rectangles or four triangles.

72

# Partitioning Rectangles

You can **partition** rectangles into equal parts using rows and columns. This rectangle has 3 rows and 3 columns, which creates 9 equal parts.

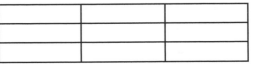

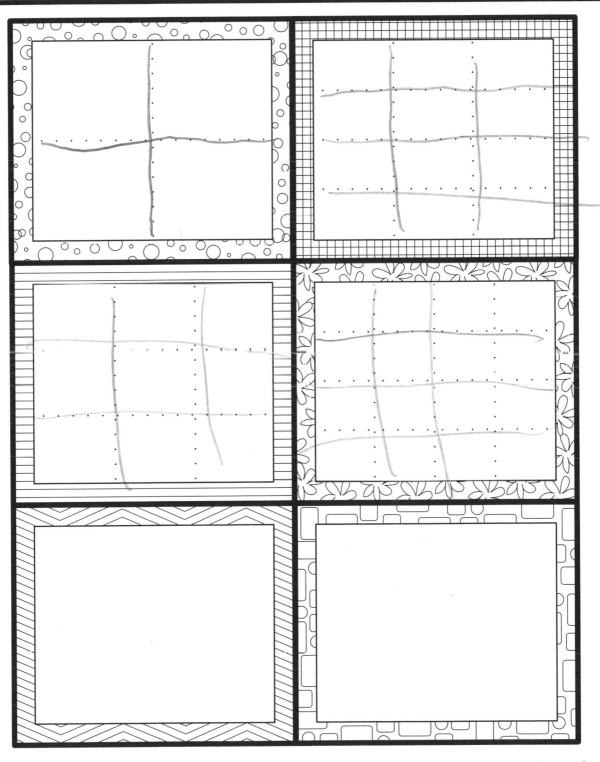

# Partitioning Shapes

## Introduction

Review the word *partition*. Give students square sheets of paper and have them cut them into two equal parts. (They may need to fold them into halves first and cut on the creases.) Ask students what they would call the two parts of the whole (halves). Repeat the activity with two more squares, dividing one into thirds and the other into fourths. Discuss how the whole can be divided into parts with different sizes and shapes, but still be equal to other wholes of the same size. Be sure students see that their two halves are the same as their three thirds, which are the same as their four fourths.

## Creating the Notebook Page

Guide students through the following steps to complete the right-hand page in their notebooks.

1. Add a Table of Contents entry for the Partitioning Shapes pages.

2. Cut out the title and glue it to the top of the page.

3. Cut out the *When shapes are partitioned* piece and glue it below the title. Complete the sentences. (Two equal parts are called **halves**. Three equal parts are called **thirds**. Four equal parts are called **fourths**.)

4. Cut out the *halves, thirds,* and *fourths* pockets. Apply glue to the back of the tabs and attach them to the bottom of the page.

5. Cut out the six shapes. Fold them on the dashed lines. Discuss how many parts each shape has. Color one section of each. Point out that one part of each whole is equal to the other parts. Finally, sort the shapes into the correct pockets, depending on how many parts they are partitioned into.

6. Draw a square near each pocket. Partition each square into halves, thirds, or fourths. Color and label one section of each square.

## Reflect on Learning

To complete the left-hand page, have students describe three different real-world scenarios where they might need to partition something into equal parts. Some examples may include dividing a cake at a party or cutting a length of tape into smaller pieces for a craft project.

# Partitioning Shapes

When shapes are **partitioned**, or divided into **equal parts**, we call the parts by special names.

half —→ 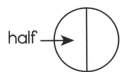    third —→     fourth —→

Two **equal parts** are called _____.
Three **equal parts** are called _____.
Four **equal parts** are called _____.

halves          thirds          fourths

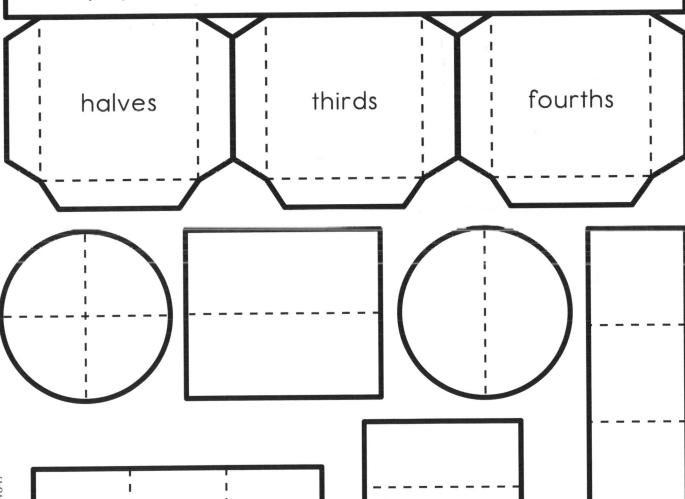

# Symmetry

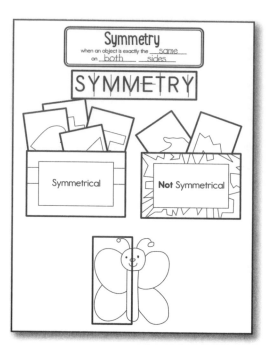

## Introduction

Explain to students that to have symmetry, an object must be the same on both sides. Hang up a picture of a large butterfly, a construction paper heart, and a bicycle. Draw a line down the center of each. Ask students which objects are the same on each side. Discuss which objects are symmetrical and how the lines show whether an object has symmetry. Then, ask students to look around the room for other objects that have symmetry. These may include a clock, books, or computer screens.

## Creating the Notebook Page

Guide students through the following steps to complete the right-hand page in their notebooks.

1. Add a Table of Contents entry for the Symmetry pages.

2. Cut out the title and glue it to the top of the page.

3. Complete the definition of *symmetry* (when an object is exactly the **same** on **both sides**).

4. Cut out the *SYMMETRY* piece and glue it below the title.

5. Draw lines on the letters in the *SYMMETRY* piece to show the letters that have symmetry.

6. Cut out the *Symmetrical* and *Not Symmetrical* pieces. Apply glue to the back of the bottom, left, and right edges of each, and attach them to the middle of the page to create pockets.

7. Cut out the six object cards. Try to draw a line of symmetry. Sort the objects into the correct pockets by determining which have symmetry and which do not. Discuss how some of the objects can have more than one line of symmetry.

8. Cut out the butterfly piece and attach it to the center of the bottom of the page. Draw the other half of the butterfly by mirroring the half image.

## Reflect on Learning

To complete the left-hand page, have students find the rest of the capital letters that have symmetry. Students should draw large capital letters and draw a line or lines of symmetry through each symmetrical letter (A, B, C, D, E, H, I, K, M, O, T, U, V, W, X).

# Symmetry

when an object is exactly the _____

on _____ _____

# SYMMETRY

Symmetrical

**Not** Symmetrical

# Tabs

Cut out each tab and label it. Apply glue to the back of each tab and align it on the outside edge of the page with only the label section showing beyond the edge. Then, fold each tab to seal the page inside.

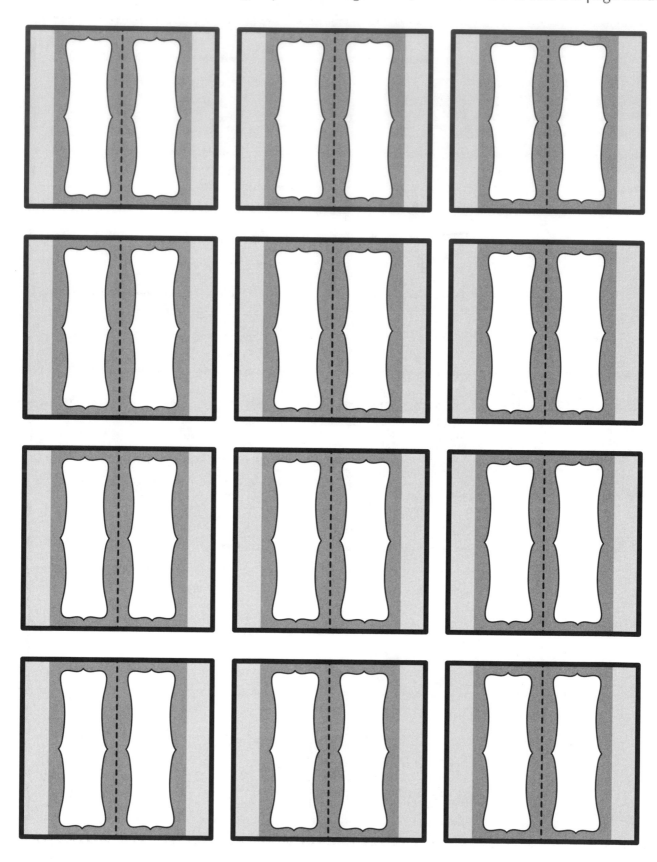

Cut out the KWL chart and cut on the solid lines to create three separate flaps. Apply glue to the back of the Topic section to attach the chart to a notebook page.

What I

# Know

What I

# Wonder

What I

# Learned

Topic: _____

# Library Pocket

Cut out the library pocket on the solid lines. Fold in the side tabs and apply glue to them before folding up the front of the pocket. Apply glue to the back of the pocket to attach it to a notebook page.

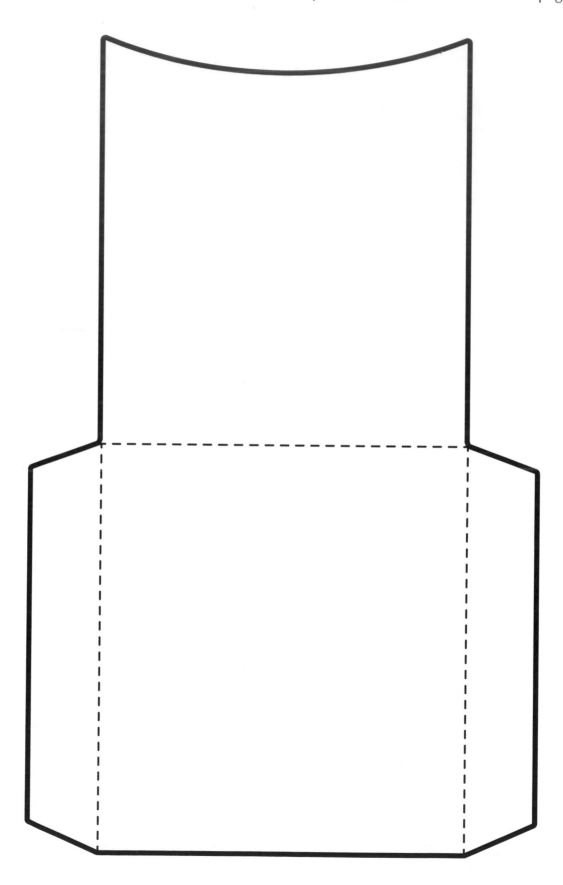

# Envelope

Cut out the envelope on the solid lines. Fold in the side tabs and apply glue to them before folding up the rectangular front of the envelope. Fold down the triangular flap to close the envelope. Apply glue to the back of the envelope to attach it to a notebook page.

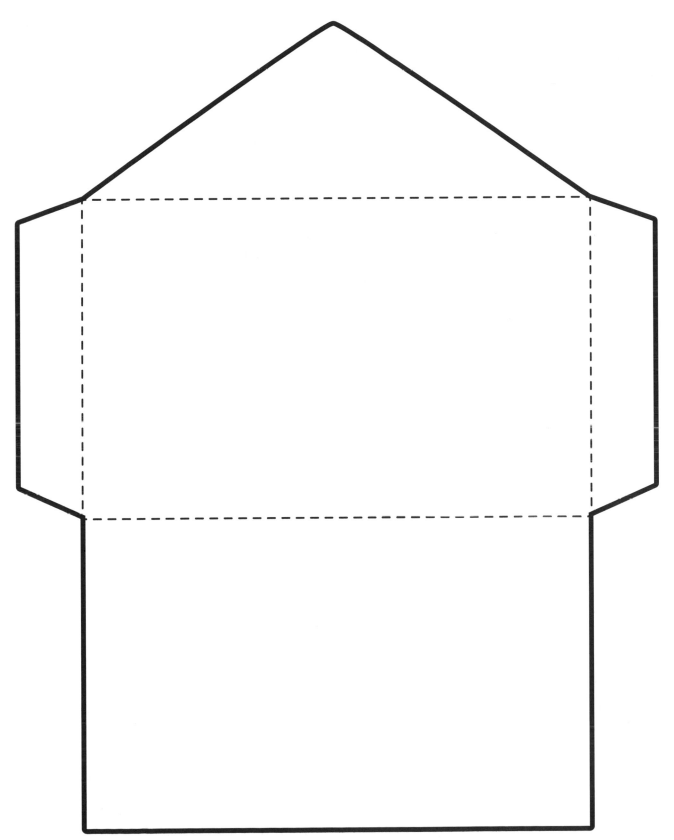

# Pocket and Cards

Cut out the pocket on the solid lines. Fold over the front of the pocket. Then, apply glue to the tabs and fold them around the back of the pocket. Apply glue to the back of the pocket to attach it to a notebook page. Cut out the cards and store them in the envelope.

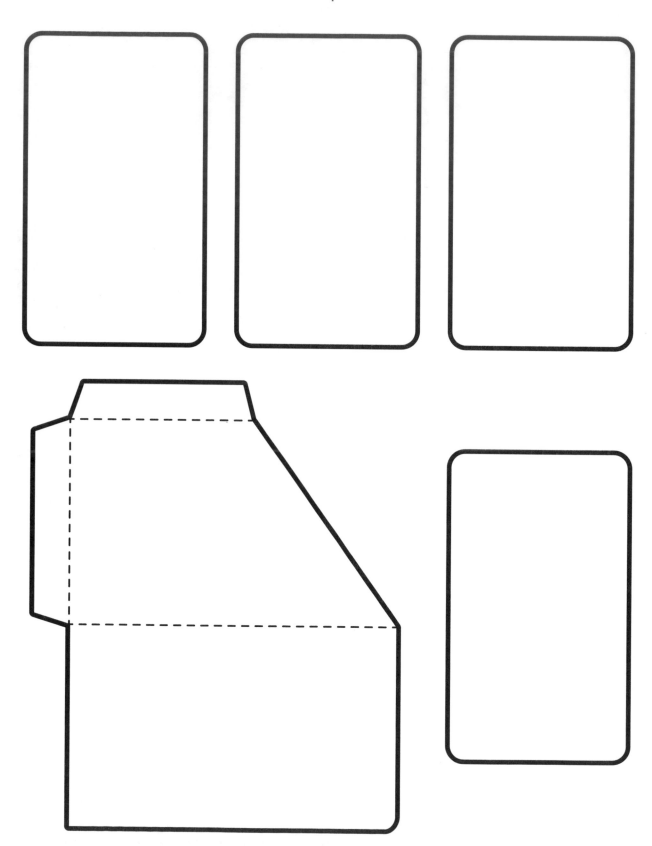

# Six-Flap Shutter Fold

Cut out the shutter fold around the outside border. Then, cut on the solid lines to create six flaps. Fold the flaps toward the center. Apply glue to the back of the shutter fold to attach it to a notebook page.

If desired, this template can be modified to create a four-flap shutter fold by cutting off the bottom row. You can also create two three-flap books by cutting it in half down the center line.

# Eight-Flap Shutter Fold

Cut out the shutter fold around the outside border. Then, cut on the solid lines to create eight flaps. Fold the flaps toward the center. Apply glue to the back of the shutter fold to attach it to a notebook page.

If desired, this template can be modified to create two four-flap shutter folds by cutting off the bottom two rows. You can also create two four-flap books by cutting it in half down the center line.

# Flap Book—Eight Flaps

Cut out the flap book around the outside border. Then, cut on the solid lines to create eight flaps. Apply glue to the back of the center section to attach it to a notebook page.

If desired, this template can be modified to create a six-flap or two four-flap books by cutting off the bottom row or two. You can also create a tall four-flap book by cutting off the flaps on the left side.

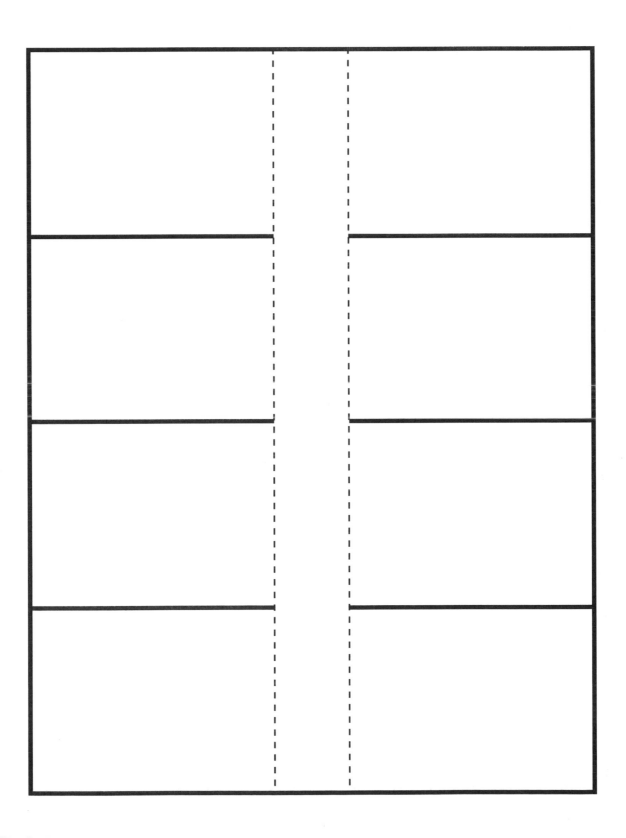

# Flap Book—Twelve Flaps

Cut out the flap book around the outside border. Then, cut on the solid lines to create 12 flaps. Apply glue to the back of the center section to attach it to a notebook page.

If desired, this template can be modified to create smaller flap books by cutting off any number of rows from the bottom. You can also create a tall flap book by cutting off the flaps on the left side.

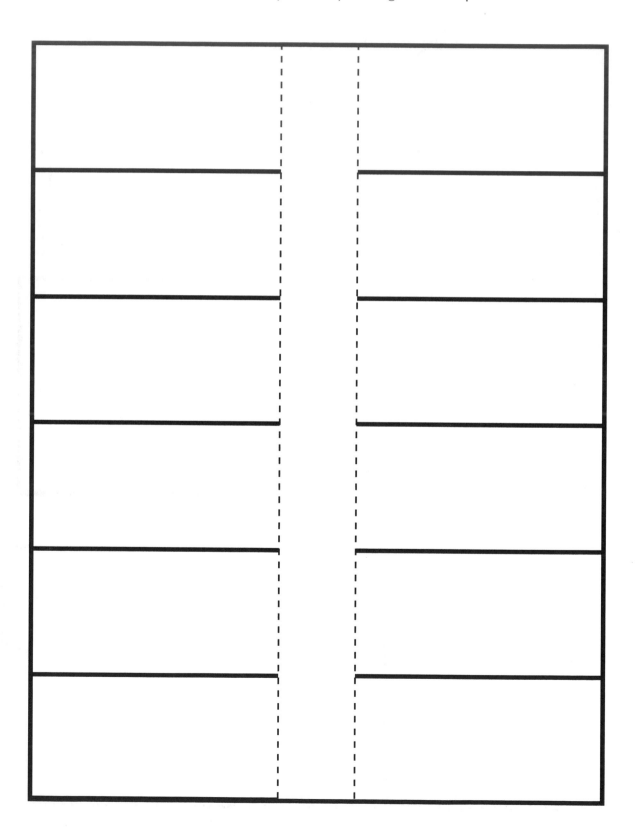

# Shaped Flaps

Cut out each shaped flap. Apply glue to the back of the narrow section to attach it to a notebook page.

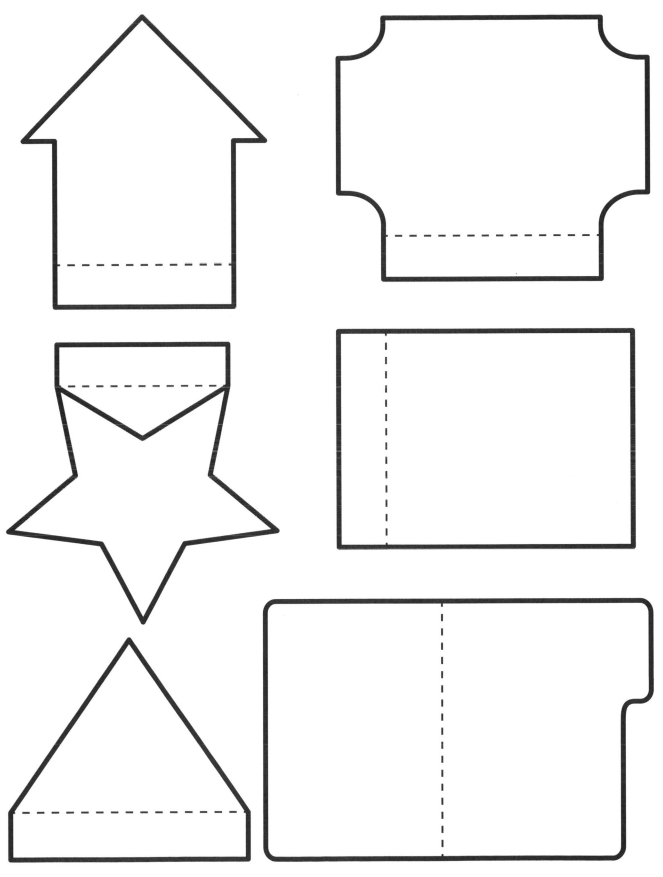

# Shaped Flaps

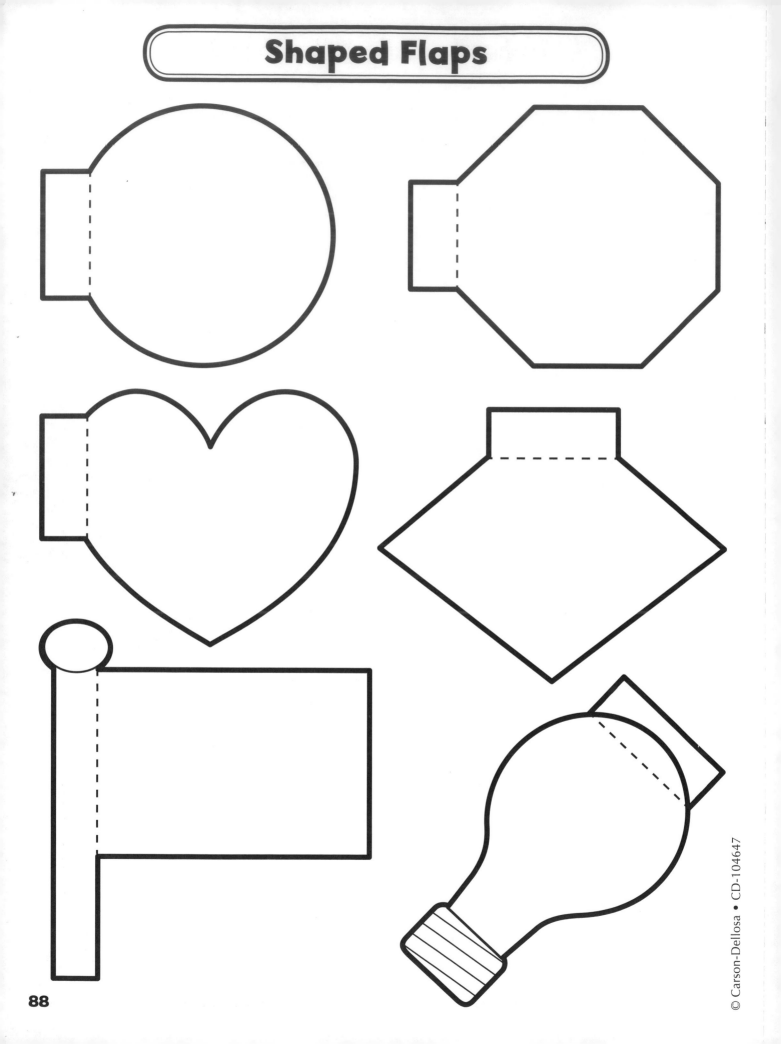

# Interlocking Booklet

Cut out the booklet on the solid lines, including the short vertical lines on the top and bottom flaps. Then, fold the top and bottom flaps toward the center, interlocking them using the small vertical cuts. Apply glue to the back of the center panel to attach it to a notebook page.

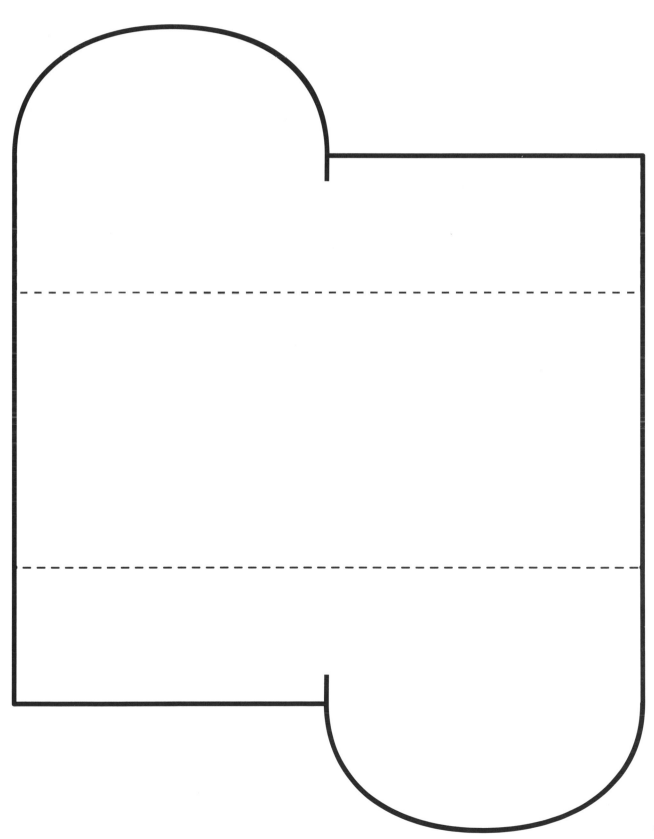

# Four-Flap Petal Fold

Cut out the shape on the solid lines. Then, fold the flaps toward the center. Apply glue to the back of the center panel to attach it to a notebook page.

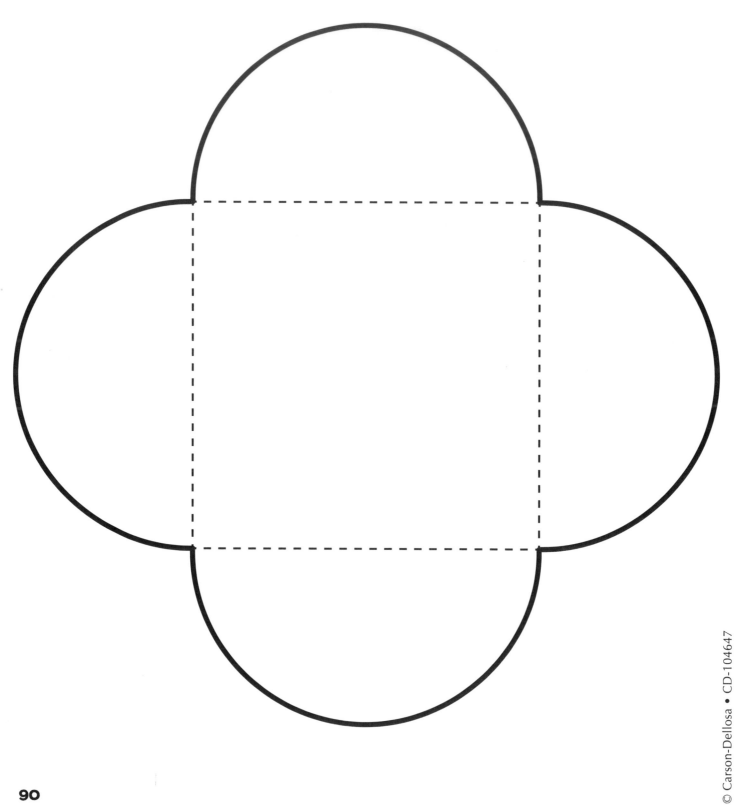

# Six-Flap Petal Fold

Cut out the shape on the solid lines. Then, fold the flaps toward the center and back out. Apply glue to the back of the center panel to attach it to a notebook page.

# Accordion Folds

Cut out the accordion pieces on the solid lines. Fold on the dashed lines, alternating the fold direction. Apply glue to the back of the last section to attach it to a notebook page.

You may modify the accordion books to have more or fewer pages by cutting off extra pages or by having students glue the first and last panels of two accordion books together.

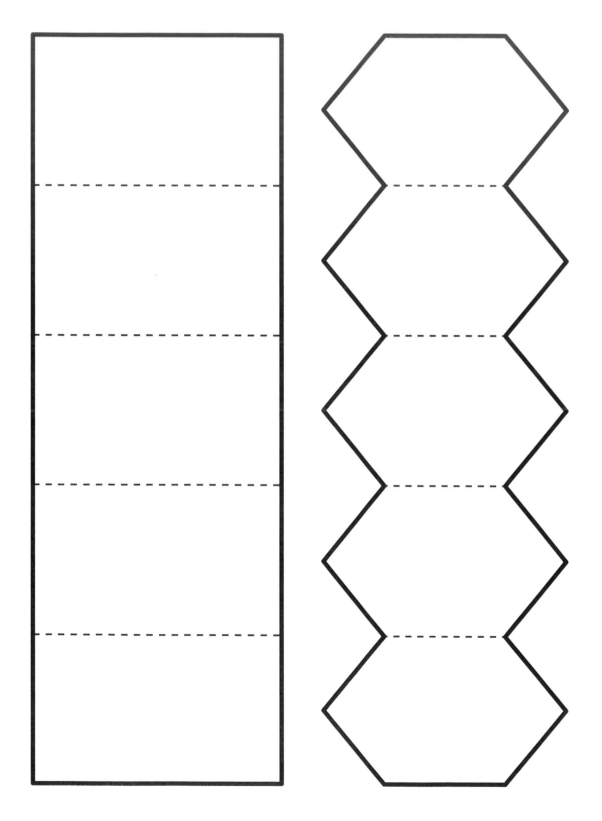

# Accordion Folds

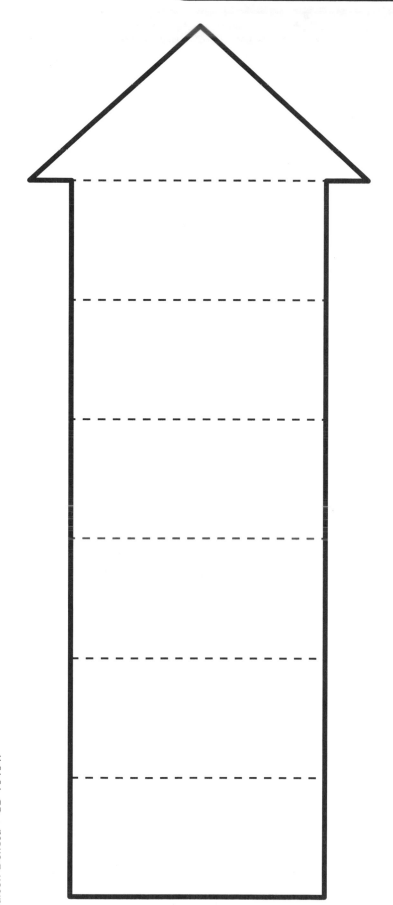

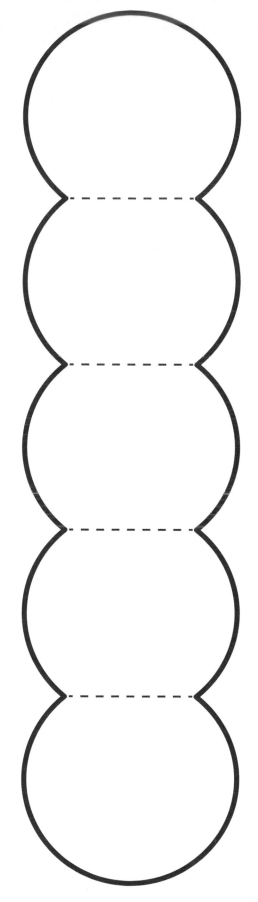

# Clamshell Fold

Cut out the clamshell fold on the solid lines. Fold and unfold the piece on the three dashed lines. With the piece oriented so that the folds form an X with a horizontal line through it, pull the left and right sides together at the fold line. Then, keeping the sides touching, bring the top edge down to meet the bottom edge. You should be left with a triangular shape that unfolds into a square. Apply glue to the back of the triangle to attach the clamshell to a notebook page.

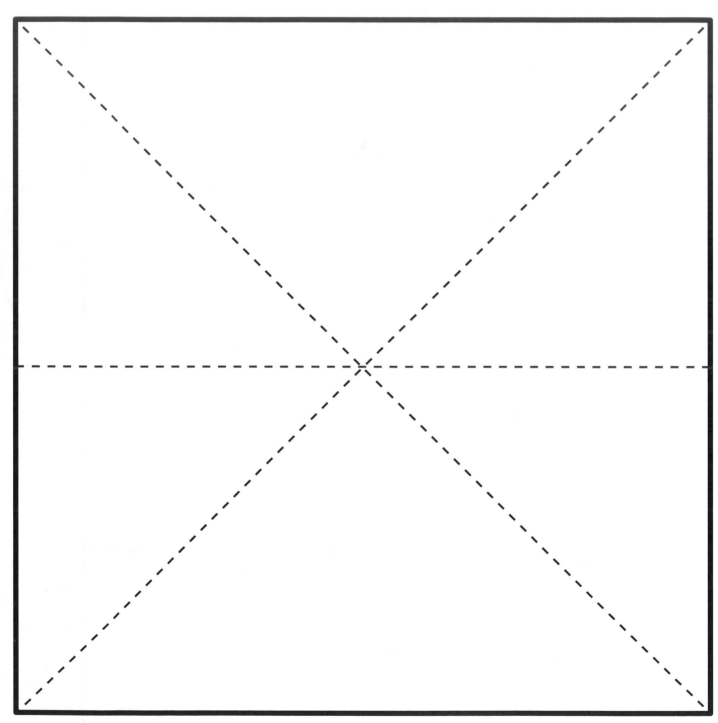

# Puzzle Pieces

Cut out each puzzle along the solid lines to create a three- or four-piece puzzle. Apply glue to the back of each puzzle piece to attach it to a notebook page. Alternately, apply glue only to one edge of each piece to create flaps.

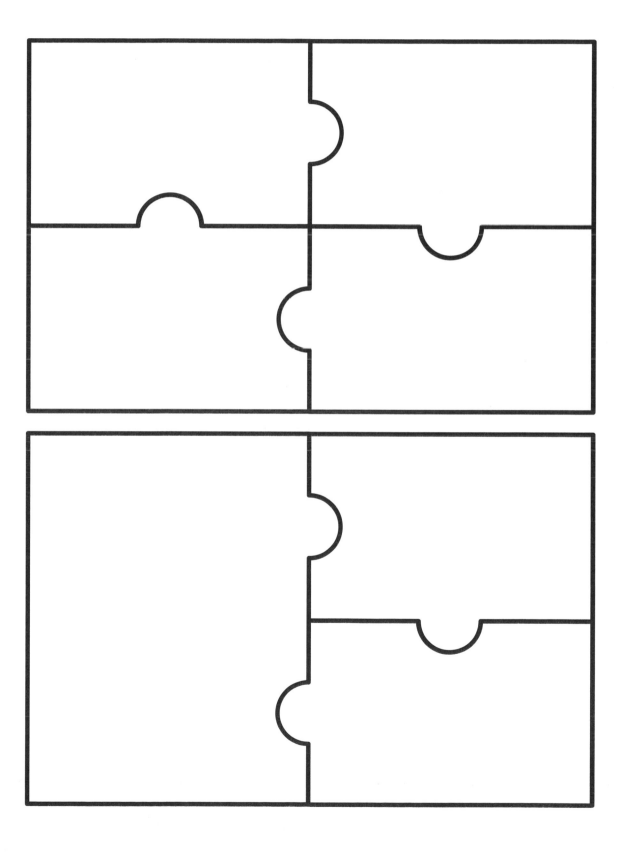

# Flip Book

Cut out the two rectangular pieces on the solid lines. Fold each rectangle on the dashed lines. Fold the piece with the gray glue section so that it is inside the fold. Apply glue to the gray glue section and place the other folded rectangle on top so that the folds are nested and create a book with four cascading flaps. Make sure that the inside pages are facing up so that the edges of both pages are visible. Apply glue to the back of the book to attach it to a notebook page.

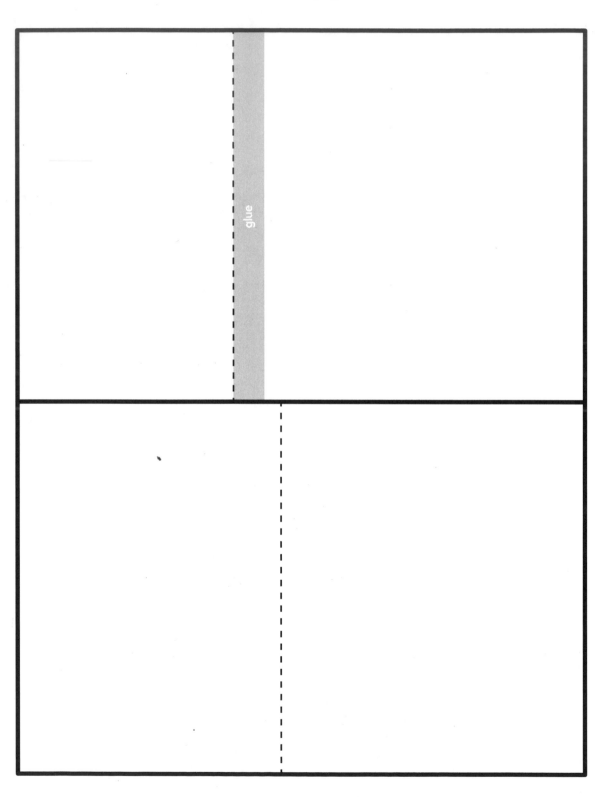